Sustainability
Micro Case Studies
for the Food Industry

Working to Make a Better Tomorrow

David McGiverin & Pamela Barrow

2nd Edition

Published by: Northwest Food Processors Association

Copyright © 2016 Northwest Food Processors Association
All rights reserved.

ISBN: 1539141713
ISBN-13: 9781539141716

8338 NE Alderwood Road, Suite 160
Portland, Oregon 97220
http://www.nwfpa.org

Book Authors:
   David McGiverin, Northwest Food Processors Association
   Pamela Barrow, Northwest Food Processors Association

Contributing Author: Josh Monifi, Northwest Food Processors Association

Contributors:
   Jennifer Ruwart, JR Collaborations
   Daniel Burgard, Cascade Earth Sciences

Cover Design: Marbry Walker, http://www.marbrywalker.com

Guidance:
   ConAgra Foods Lamb Weston (Paul Halberstadt)
   Del Monte Foods (Robin Connell & John Wisse)
   National Frozen Foods Corporation (Amyris Borgo)
   Oregon Cherry Growers, Inc. (Steve Kollars)
   J.R. Simplot Company (Alan Prouty)
   Tillamook County Creamery Association (Shawn Reiersgaard)
   Tree Top, Inc. (Chris Cary)
   Truitt Bros., Inc. (Heather McPherson)

This work was supported by a Specialty Crop Block Grant from the Washington State Department of Agriculture, Idaho Department of Agriculture and the Oregon Department of Agriculture. Some materials are based upon work supported by the Hitachi Foundation.

For additional information, contact:
   sustainability@nwfpa.org
   503.327.2200
   http://www.nwfpa.org/sustainability

Contents:

Disclaimer i

Forward iii

Introduction v

SECTION ONE   SOCIAL SUSTAINABILITY 1

Life Skills Training for Immigrant Workers Benefits
Employees and Employer 7

On-Site Health Clinic Improves Employee Health
and Reduces Health Care Costs 9

Voluntary Full Safety Compliance Reduces Injuries and
Premiums 11

Create a Formal Process to Recognize Employees' Efforts 13

Cultivate Managers and Leaders by Providing
Educational Opportunities 15

Photo ID Badges Personalize the Workplace 17

Training for Special Needs Individuals Produces
Skilled and Dedicated Workers 19

Partnership with Oregon Food Bank Drives Hunger Relief 21

On-Site Childcare and Tutoring 23

Helping Employees with Their Own Recycling 25

Donating Reusable Items Cuts Down on Waste and

Helps the Community 27

Energy Fairs Save Energy at Home and at Work 29

Smart Commuter Helps Employees Reduce

Their Carbon Footprints 32

Green Machine Program Encourages

Employees to Use Alternative Transportation 34

PART TWO   ENVIRONMENTAL SUSTAINABILITY 37

Automatic Flow Controls Save Water and Reduce Costs 41

Comprehensive Assessment and Plan Reduce

Water Use by 24% 43

Screen Solids and Use Low-Flow Spray Bars to

Reduce Wastewater Costs 45

Low Capital and Behavioral Changes Reduce

Wastewater Discharges by 19% 47

Rejuvenate Engineered Wetlands for More

Effective Nutrient Recycling 49

Re-piping and Water Recycling Reduces Water

Use and Energy Costs 51

Automatic Solenoid Valves Assure Water Used

Only When Needed 53

Water Use Reduction and Wasted Product Recovery 55

Boiler Piping Improvements Reduce Water and Energy Consumption 57

Onsite Waste Water Treatment and Biogas Recovery Reduce Sewer Fees and Energy Costs 59

Reduced Water Use, Discharge and Solids Decrease Water Costs and Wastewater Fees......................... 61

Sustainable Farming Practices, Solar Power, Recycling and Rail.. 65

Bioswales Remove Pollution from Surface Water Runoff......... 68

Composting and Recycle Sorting Reduce Waste and Disposal Costs 70

Recycling and Recovery Reduce Waste Disposal Fees and Generate Revenue 72

Reusable and Returnable Bags Reduce Paper Waste 74

Composting Reduces Waste and Landfill Costs 76

HotRot Composter Reduces Organic Waste and Produces Soil Amendments for Agricultural Application 78

Rail Transfer Facility Allows Greater Use of More Efficient and Cleaner Rail Transportation 80

Sonic Air Dryers More Energy Efficient than Compressed Air Dryers 82

Energy Efficiency Results in Stable Energy Costs Even with Increased Production... 84

Lighting Retrofit of Old System Reduces Energy Costs............ 86

Solar Power Reduces Demand Charges and Supplies
Part of Power Needs 88

Energy Efficient Air Compressor Project
Produces Significant Energy Savings... 91

Tracking and Analyzing Water Use Reveals Hidden Leaks...... 93

Reducing kWh with a Fan VFD and Pump
System Automation.. 95

Eliminating Negative Air Conveyance Saves
Energy and Maintenance... 97

Heat Reclaim on Corn Processing Line Saves Energy 99

Lighting Upgrades Produce Big Savings
and Improved Visibility... 101

Innovative Packaging Eliminates Crates and
Allows Direct Palletizing 103

Eliminating Chemicals and Reducing
Blowdown in Cooling Tower Maintenance 105

Technology Reduces Scale on Apples and
Increases Profits... 108

Diverting Waste Saves Money and Reduces
Environmental Impacts... 110

Lighting Replacements and Strategic Energy Management
Deliver Significant Energy Savings.. 112

Eliminating Redundant Uses Saves Water 114

Partnerships to Repurpose Waxed Cardboard.. 116

Consolidating Vendors' Shipments Reduces Number of Deliveries and Greenhouse Gas Emissions 118

Successful Implementation of Process Wastewater Recycling 120

Engaging Industrial Partners to Support Composting of Organic Waste Byproducts 124

Thinking Outside the Canister for Low-Impact Packaging 127

Shore Power Electricity for Trailer Refrigeration 129

District Energy for Food Manufacturers is Energy Efficient and Low Carbon 132

PART THREE   ECONOMIC SUSTAINABILITY 135

Employee-Driven Continuous Improvement 140

Community-based On-Site Ammonia Safety Training 142

Employee Workforce Referral Pipeline 144

Communicating the Vision to Employees 146

Financial Literacy Program Reduces Employee Stress 148

A Living Wage for All Employees Boosts Productivity 150

Partner with State Employment Training to Reduce Training Costs and Increase Employee Skills 152

Employee Training Improves Productivity and Employee Retention 154

Mechanical Separation of Packaging from Food Wastes
allows Recycling and Eliminates Disposal Fees...................... 156

In-sourcing Ingredients Improves Quality and
Engages Employees... 158

Onsite Agriculture Supplies High Quality and
Sustainable Raw Materials.. 160

Biodiesel from Spent Vegetable Oil Offsets
Petroleum Fuels Use 162

On-site Electric Vehicle Charging Stations............................. 164

Green Teams Drive Recycling Program Successes............... 166

Annual Energy Program Assessments and
Awards Boost Achievement.. 168

Photos Raise Employee Awareness of Waste
Reduction Opportunities... 170

Celebrating Wins and Communicating Success
through Videos 172

Fair Game, Fair Match, Fair Trade+ 174

Screen Displays Provide Real-Time Energy
Monitoring for Production Personnel 176

CRES-Certified Employees Drive Efficient Equipment
Operations and Energy Savings.. 178

Disclaimer

This book is designed to provide information and motivation to our readers. The content of each case study reflects the experience and the results of the reporting company. NWFPA and the publisher make no representations or warranties of any kind and assume no liabilities of any kind with respect to the application of the contents and specifically disclaim any fitness of use for a particular purpose or expected results. Neither NWFPA nor the publisher shall be responsible to any person or entity with respect to any loss or incidental or consequential damages caused or alleged to have been caused, directly or indirectly, by the information or actions contained herein. Every company is different and the ideas and strategies contained herein may not be suitable for your situation. You should seek the services of a competent professional before beginning any improvement program.

Forward

This is the second edition of our 2013 publication *Sustainability Micro Case Studies for Food Processors: Working to Make a Better Tomorrow*. We changed the title slightly (from "processors" to "industry") for this second edition to reflect that case studies from suppliers and customers of food processors are included as well as food processor case studies. These other organizations are part of the food industry and sustainable practices throughout the supply chain contribute to the sustainability of the overall industry.

This second edition contains the original case studies, many of which have been updated to reflect changes and/or more recent results since the first edition. Further, 28 new case studies have been added.

Northwest Food Processors Association (NWFPA) sincerely thanks all those organizations who contributed their case studies to this publication. These are real activities with actual documented results that have been implemented by the food industry. Our industry is committed to incorporating sustainability into our business practices. The industry is aggressively taking actions to become more sustainable. Many people, however, are not aware of the industry's sustainability accomplishments. We appreciate the willingness of the case study contributors to share their issues and challenges, solutions and results so that we can raise awareness of these important activities and achievements throughout the food industry and with the public.

David McGiverin

President, Northwest Food Processors Association

Pamela Barrow

Vice President, Energy, Environmental & Sustainability, Northwest Food Processors Association

Introduction

While there are many definitions of sustainability, it has become the catchword of the decade. Over time, "sustainability" has evolved from a mere catchword to a full-fledged business concept that is being embraced by more and more companies, can increase profitability, and reduce environmental impacts and enhance social responsibility.

Many companies are developing sustainability programs to guide their sustainability efforts. A robust sustainability program can be thought of as a three-legged stool, with environmental (planet), economic (profit) and social (people) issues each representing a leg of the stool. These three legs are often referred to as the "triple bottom line."

The environmental leg represents efforts to balance the use of limited resources today with the resource needs of tomorrow. Environmental sustainability addresses such topics as energy, water use, invasive species, genetically modified seeds, chemical fertilizers, soil erosion, and the preservation of farmland.

The economic sustainability leg of the stool focuses on issues which allow business to thrive in both the community and the marketplace. Economic sustainability initiatives return a profit to shareholders or cooperative members, develop value-added products, establish market share, eliminate artificial barriers to business, and work to establish a level playing field in the marketplace.

The third leg, social responsibility, involves a company's role in supporting a healthy and secure workforce and investing in the community through taxes, leadership, social justice, and philanthropy.

In 2010 the Northwest Food Processors Association (NWFPA) adopted the 1987 Brundtland Commission definition of Sustainability that states:

> *Sustainable development is development that meets the needs of the present without compromising the ability of future generations to meet their own needs.*

Based on this foundational definition, NWFPA set its objective to "mainstream sustainability in the food processing industry" and help food companies incorporate sustainability into their business practices. To further this objective, NWFPA creates frameworks, guidance, and resources that food companies can use in developing individual company sustainability programs and plans.

NWFPA developed this book as a vehicle for food companies to share real life sustainability practices and actions they are taking to become more sustainable. It is also designed to be a catalyst to inspire companies to take action and adopt new and better ways of doing business. The intent is that readers will identify ideas and actions that they can modify and implement in their own facilities.

The book is divided into three sections and each section addresses one of the three legs of sustainability: *social sustainability, environmental sustainability,* and *economic sustainability.* Each section begins with a definition and an introduction explaining the elements of the individual "leg." The body of the section presents the various practices, actions or approaches that were submitted by individual companies.

Food companies have a long history of finding ways to become more sustainable and they value continuous improvements to these efforts. They realize that sustainability is good for the community, the environment, and long-term economic viability.

These values are best expressed through the Northwest Food Processors Association's Sustainability Statement:

> *The food processing industry has been, and continues to be, an integral part of the Northwest economy for over a century. Continued viability of our industry will be dependent on the success of our ongoing efforts to address water, energy, safety, community, and environmental responsibilities.*
>
> *—Northwest Food Processors Association*
> *Sustainability Task Force, 2010*

In 2016, NWFPA adopted a Sustainability Philosophy in its Public Policy Book:

> *NWFPA advocates for policies and programs that contribute to sustainability, whether the issue is food safety, energy, environmental, workforce or tax policies. Sustainability*

is the overarching philosophy that guides our efforts in all areas of concern. Sustainable practices ensure the continued viability of the food industry.

The question for food companies today is not *if*, but *how* they should manage their sustainability activities.

ABOUT NORTHWEST FOOD PROCESSORS ASSOCIATION

Formed in 1914, and headquartered in Portland, Oregon, the Northwest Food Processors Association (NWFPA) serves as an advocate for the interests of its members and as a resource for enhancing their competitive capabilities. NWFPA's membership includes national companies with facilities in the Pacific Northwest, regional companies and locally run businesses. NWFPA is one of the largest food industry trade associations, with current membership of more than 150 food processor companies with over 250 facilities and more than 350 supplier members. Primary members are located in the states of Idaho, Oregon and Washington; with affiliate members located outside the Northwest and in Canada.

NWFPA focuses its efforts on policy, technical, regulatory and advocacy in the major issues impacting the food processing industry: Energy, Environmental, Government Affairs, Operations & Technical, Sustainability and Workforce. NWFPA members provide advice and guide association activities and priorities through participation in committees and task forces in these issue areas. NWFPA is governed by a board of directors elected by the membership.

NWFPA delivers information, training, tools and resources on important matters affecting the food industry. A primary vehicle is the annual Northwest Food Manufacturing & Packaging Exposition and Conference. Held in January, it is the largest regional food manufacturing tradeshow in North America and attracts food industry professionals and suppliers from across the country. In addition to featuring nearly 500 exhibitor booths, the event offers a comprehensive program of leading-edge educational sessions.

Events specifically related to sustainability include the annual Sustainability Summit, held in Portland in mid-April and the annual NW Industrial Energy Efficiency Summit co-located with the Exposition and Conference. The Sustainability Summit brings together food companies, sustainability experts and industry partners working to advance sustainability in the food industry. Sessions are focused on practical industrial applications of sustainability management practices. For information see **www.nwfpa.org/sustainabilitysummit.**

The NW Industrial Energy Efficiency Summit, produced by NWFPA in conjunction with the Northwest's major energy organizations, is the region's premier gathering of industries and energy interests working to advance industrial competitiveness through energy efficiency. Sessions focus on practical applications of energy efficient technologies in both electricity and natural gas and energy management approaches with energy experts and industry personnel presenting real-life energy savings success stories and challenges. The Energy Summit is now in its ninth year. For information see **www.nwfpa.org/energysummit.**

For additional information about NWFPA, educational resources, events, or membership, see www.nwfpa.org or contact:

info@nwfpa.org or call **503-327-2200.**

NWFPA SUSTAINABILITY PROGRAM

Northwest Food Processors Association (NWFPA) leadership identified Sustainability as a key strategic priority for the food industry. NWFPA's sustainability efforts began with the formation of a Sustainability Task Force charged with defining sustainability from a food industry perspective, guiding the development of a framework and identifying resources necessary to help mainstream sustainability throughout the region's food industry.

In 2010, NWFPA adopted the following widely accepted definition of sustainability:

Sustainable development is development that meets the needs of the present without compromising the ability of future generations to meet their own needs.

(Bruntland Commission 1987)

In 2012, NWFPA launched a major sustainability initiative and the NWFPA board of directors elevated the Sustainability Task Force to standing committee status in the association. The new Sustainability Committee's membership was broadened to include representatives of NWFPA's five other standing committees. This echoes the contemporary approach to sustainability as the umbrella under which many areas of effort fall, including energy, water, waste, greenhouse gas emissions, workforce, and community involvement. Broader participation assures development of products and services that will provide resources for NWFPA members in their sustainability efforts.

SUSTAINABILITY FACTORS

The NWFPA Task Force identified the following as important factors to be considered in developing and implementing a sustainability program:

- Continuous availability of resources including water, land and energy products at sustainable levels, quality and cost;
- Acknowledgement of sustainability as a factor in consumer purchasing preferences; positive business and brand recognition associated with our products which are recognized as sustainable by consumers;
- Implementing sustainability is challenging and complex, especially measurement and reporting and supply chain effects;
- Importance of participating in public, legislative and regulatory arenas that can impact or influence sustainable practices;
- Sustainability performance can impact the ability of employers to attract and maintain high-performing talent; and

- Honest reporting and communications on sustainability efforts.

SUSTAINABILITY RESOURCES

The following resources are available for download on the NWFPA web site at **www.nwfpa.org** and their development was funded by a Specialty Crop Block Grant from the Oregon Department of Agriculture, Washington Department of Agriculture, and the Idaho Department of Agriculture:

- ***Sustainability Guide*** — provides a resource that assists companies in the development of an individualized sustainability program to meet the needs of their companies, their communities and their consumers.
- ***Water Sustainability Training Course*** — provides three training modules to educate food company personnel about the importance of water sustainability and the activities that are performed to achieve efficient water use.
- ***Sustainability Micro Case Studies for Food Processors*** — presents real-life sustainability actions and approaches that are designed to provide ideas for sustainability efforts and to inspire others to apply in their own organizations.
- **NWFPA's Energy Roadmap for Members** charts a suggested path for individual food companies to achieve energy intensity reductions. Companies can use the Roadmap as a guide for setting energy intensity goals and for developing a strategic energy management plan or action plan for their facilities. It also includes a self-assessment to help companies gauge their current level of energy efficiency efforts and identify actions that could

allow them to operate at a higher level of efficiency. The appendices include supporting information as well as valuable resource contacts. This work was supported by the Northwest Energy Efficiency Alliance.

Visit the Sustainability pages on the NWFPA web site at www.nwfpa.org to obtain downloadable versions of sustainability resources for the food processing industry.

SECTION ONE

SOCIAL SUSTAINABILITY

Social Sustainability is the positive effect that a company has on society through community investment. This includes providing safe and nutritious food, safe jobs, and community development."

—*Northwest Food Processors Sustainability Guide*

INTRODUCING SOCIAL SUSTAINABILITY

In the Northwest, the food industry has a significant influence on the economic health of surrounding communities, especially in rural areas. Key economic activities include the farming, harvesting, processing, and distribution of agricultural and natural resource products. These activities provide direct and indirect employment as well as opportunities for people to engage in community services. Employees serve as volunteer firefighters, Little League coaches, teacher assistants, choir members, and scout leaders. A company that understands its ties to a community promotes a vibrant workforce when it provides employees opportunities to give back to the community. This relationship among the company, its employees, and the community instills trust, pride, and loyalty. Bright futures for a company and its community are inextricably intertwined.

Quality of life is important for employee and community wellbeing. A living-wage job with opportunities for personal development and employee engagement within a safe and supportive environment are essential for good morale. Happy employees take pride in what they do, are healthier, and have good social relationships—and this spirit spills over into the entire community.

Food safety is a major public concern and is a priority of food companies. It is the "product responsibility" of the food industry, and poorly handled prevention and response can erode trust in a company's products. USDA and FDA regulations are extremely complex, and companies direct significant resources toward compliance. Support of research on better and quicker pathogen detection methods and new and safer processing and packaging will promote greater safety and consumer trust in the industry.

Community outreach demonstrates a company's vested interest in its community. Outreach efforts include partnering with community programs like community cleanup, charitable giving, or empowering those in need, providing vocational educational opportunities like internships, apprenticeships, or tours for schools, and delivering general skills training for employees, such as learning a new language, health/safety certifications, or technology courses. These can be achieved by offering incentives and/or time for employees to pursue their passions, while providing forums for employees to share ideas and work together.

Questions to Ask

- What is your company doing to engage and empower employees?
- Do employees at your company have opportunities to learn and grow?
- What values/interests/passions does your company share with the local community?

- What role can your company play in the local community?
- Do you have programs to encourage employee volunteerism?

Life Skills Training for Immigrant Workers Benefits Employees and Employer

Bellingham Cold Storage

OPPORTUNITY

Gayle Davis teaches English to immigrant employees at Bellingham Cold Storage (BCS). She noticed that her students faced many challenges in being new to the United States besides language that impacted their ability to perform at full potential.

SOLUTION

Employees now learn the basics of living in the United States as part of their English classes, including how to use US currency, shop for familiar foods and necessities, communicate with families back home, and navigate situational experiences, such as attending a child's parent-teacher conference.

RESULTS

Since adding life skills to the English classes to help employees overcome personal issues, BCS has seen increased employee morale and Improved employee health. There have also been positive outcomes for the company including increased quality and production, and reduced absenteeism and turnover.

The program also creates a strong internal labor pool for recruiting and promoting, and a robust employee referral pipeline because employees feel valued and cared for. The company gains a reputation as a great place to work, attracting the best talent in the area.

On-Site Health Clinic Improves Employee Health and Reduces Health Care Costs

Bellingham Cold Storage

OPPORTUNITY

In the mid-2000s Bellingham Cold Storage (BCS) became a self-insured company, saving the company $400,000 to $600,000 annually. Even with this dramatic cost savings, BCS still wondered how it might better manage its health care costs while improving the overall health of its employees.

A cost analysis indicated that it may be more cost-efficient for BCS to run its own on-site clinic. This could also address many of the barriers to care that increase use of emergency care:

- Availability of appointments
- Location of services
- Finding a trusted health-care provider
- Co-pays that felt prohibitively high

SOLUTION

BCS decided to proceed with an on-site clinic. Since BCS itself did not have enough potential patients to make a clinic viable, it invited one of its tenants, Trans-Ocean Products, to become a partner in the health care clinic, called the M*i*Care Clinic.

Now, employees of both companies have access to on-site, high-quality, personalized care at no cost. Employees and their dependents can make 20-minute appointments with no waiting and no co-pay. The clinic's pharmacy stocks over 100 medications, which are provided to patients also without co-pay for the first 90 days of a prescription.

RESULTS

Both BCS and Trans-Ocean Products say that it is too early to tell but are confident they will see healthier employees and lower costs. Because employees primarily access care when they are sick, BCS and Trans-Ocean are exploring incentives to encourage employees to focus on preventative medicine.

Voluntary Full Safety Compliance Reduces Injuries and Premiums

Henningsen Cold Storage

OPPORTUNITY

Henningsen Cold Storage (HCS) employees work in extreme temperatures and perform heavy-duty labor.

The company knows that injuries not only impact productivity but also employees' quality of life. HCS wanted a program that would help the company and its workers minimize on-the-job hazards and prevent injuries, illnesses, and deaths in the workplace.

SOLUTION

Rather than wait for the Occupational Safety and Health Administration (OSHA) to conduct an on-site inspection, which are conducted randomly and without advance notice, HCS sought OSHA's assistance to bring the company into full compliance with OSHA requirements.

RESULTS

Company leaders have made safety a daily way of doing business at HCS. Each individual location and location manager is responsible for the facility safety plan. The managers, direct reports, and safety committee execute the safety plan and all employees are actively engaged in safety. As a result of this and other practices HCS has implemented, its Experience Modification Factor (MOD) rate is .77, which is one of the lowest in the industry. The company has also attained OSHA SHARP (Safety and Health Achievement Recognition Program) certification for most of its facilities. The SHARP program was developed to recognize smaller employers who have utilized OSHA's On-site Consultation Program services to improve and maintain an exemplary injury and illness prevention program. Worksites that achieve the SHARP status are recognized by OSHA as a model employer for safety and health. In addition to fewer accidents, insurance claims have been reduced, premiums reduced, and employee satisfaction and morale has increased.

Create a Formal Process to Recognize Employees' Efforts

Green Mountain Coffee Roasters, Inc.

OPPORTUNITY

Green Mountain Coffee Roasters has a reputation as a great employer and overall employee satisfaction is consistently high. However, an annual employee survey revealed dissatisfaction with company acknowledgement and celebration of personal and professional milestones. Green Mountain desired to create a more formal process for celebrating milestones, from birthdays and employment anniversaries to the successful completion of projects, such as a software implementation.

SOLUTION

The monthly employee newsletter now includes employee birthdays and employment anniversaries, and it acknowledges employees for reaching their goals.

RESULTS

Employee recognition and celebration of personal milestones has created camaraderie among employees and goodwill between Green Mountain and its employees. It has also increased employees' personal pride in contribution and driven friendly competition as employees know that delivering superior results will be recognized.

Cultivate Managers and Leaders by Providing Educational Opportunities

Henningsen Cold Storage

OPPORTUNITY

Henningsen Cold Storage (HCS) operates in an industry with an average turnover rate of 35%. High turnover drives up recruitment and on-boarding costs and can make it challenging to cultivate an internal labor force for promotions and advancements.

SOLUTION

HCS addresses high turnover by creating a culture where managers "hire to fit" by asking "*Will this person fit within our group?*" Managers strive to *hire* for customer service and attitude and then to *train* in specific skills. Once the right candidates are hired, HCS seeks further opportunities for managers to identify and cultivate frontline workers for supervisory and manager positions.

Managers nominate employees to attend the WFLO Institute, which is an arm of the World Food Logistics Organization. If approved by the executive team, these employees attend three days of in-depth classes in cold storage, or public refrigerated warehousing, annually for three consecutive years. Employees are selected based on the following characteristics: productivity, leadership, willingness to take on increasing levels of responsibility, strong communication skills, respect and likability by management and the team, and a "make it happen" attitude.

HCS has also started a Management Trainee program in which quality individuals are identified as future leaders and work to develop them within the company culture. They learn various aspects of the company and are given opportunities to grow by experiencing different assignments within the company.

RESULTS

The WFLO training opportunities have improved employee satisfaction, loyalty, and morale and have expanded the skills of HCS employees, increasing productivity and improving customer service. WFLO is an important part of developing HCS leaders and teams. The Management Trainee program continues to identify and develop future leaders who can keep the HCS culture alive and direct the company while upholding its values.

Photo ID Badges Personalize the Workplace

Dave's Killer Bread

OPPORTUNITY

As Dave's Killer Bread grew, it became increasingly difficult for managers and leaders to remember the names of all employees. The company needed a way to help managers learn and remember the names of frontline workers as part of a continuing effort to encourage authentic connections between managers and employees.

SOLUTION

All employees now wear photo ID badges.

RESULTS

Wearing photo ID badges has made employees feel *seen*. The quality of their work has tended to improve, as they also feel more accountable. Employees also feel more valued when managers know who they are and take an interest in their work and their lives. They take more pride in their work, which has had a positive impact on productivity.

Training for Special Needs Individuals Produces Skilled and Dedicated Workers

Tim's Cascade Snacks

OPPORTUNITY

Tim's Cascade Snacks (Tim's) has been manufacturing unique potato chips and other snacks since 1986 using an old family recipe. Tim's has created a loyal and dedicated workforce through its numerous community support and outreach efforts. The company wanted a way to provide employment to the underserved and those with various disabilities.

SOLUTION

Tim's works closely with its community partners Auburn School District and Vadis Northwest to provide employment opportunities to special education students and individuals with mental, physical, or developmental disabilities. The company currently employs three trainees: one from Auburn and two from Vadis, though these numbers change from year to year.

RESULTS

The company believes that these individuals deserve a chance to earn a living wage and has experienced that they often become extremely dedicated and dependable employees. When feasible, Tim's transitions the trainees into permanent positions.

Partnership with Oregon Food Bank Drives Hunger Relief

Pacific Natural Foods and Oregon Food Bank Partnership

OPPORTUNITY

In pursuit of its core belief that no person should be hungry, Pacific Natural Foods donates to the Oregon Food Bank (OFB). But the company wanted to increase OFB services to the disadvantaged by allowing OFB to accept food and agricultural donations that otherwise could not be distributed through the OFB Network.

SOLUTION

Pacific Natural Foods developed a unique and multifaceted partnership with OFB. The company donates countless hours of production line time, labor, R&D, ingredients, and packaging to

OFB. In addition, Pacific Natural Foods encourages participation and engagement through the following programs:

- Employees volunteer at the Oregon Food Bank
- Customers encouraged to aid in hunger relief. Pacific Natural product labels express the company's commitment and encourage customers to follow its lead
- Employees giving campaign to OFB.

RESULTS

Over the past 10 years, Pacific Natural Foods has donated more than 9.4 million pounds of food to the Oregon Food Bank. In fiscal year 2011, Pacific Natural Foods donated 1.2 million pounds of food, which is equivalent to 923,077 meals.

On-Site Childcare and Tutoring

Boardman Foods, Inc.

OPPORTUNITY

Schools in Boardman, OR let out at 3 pm and parents must find childcare or leave their children at home alone until they get off work. Back in 2007, Boardman Foods, Inc. saw that many of its employees were concerned about the well-being of their children during this time. Boardman Foods wanted moms and dads to have a free safe place for their children to be during this period of time. Furthermore, Boardman Foods wanted the children of its workforce to have the opportunity to get some one-on-one after school tutoring in the areas in which they needed help.

SOLUTION

Boardman Foods' Director of Operations spoke with the school superintendent to get permission for the school bus to make a stop at the Boardman Foods plant every day. Employees are now able to pick up their children right at the facility where they work and know that their homework has been completed and a snack has been provided. Additionally, this allows the parents to enjoy evenings with their children and know their schoolwork is done. Boardman Foods management worked with local authorities to make needed adjustments to the facility to host this type of operation.

RESULTS

Boardman Foods' employees embraced this program and praised the company for providing a solution to this challenge. Around 10 smiling children arrive at the plant every day, with no behavioral issues. The after-school instructor enjoys the job and the school administration is pleased that students get the attention they need. Ease of mind helps increase employee productivity and reduces lost time needed to address child care issues. Employee stress levels are lowered knowing that their children are getting the extra attention needed to excel.

Helping Employees with Their Own Recycling

Kerr Concentrates, Inc.

OPPORTUNITY

Kerr Concentrates has been dedicated to recycling since the 1980s. But since 2009, the company's Sustainability Team has worked on adding more recycling bins and marking them for easy usage. They are even recycling items like light bulbs, electrical wire, and other difficult items. In 2014, the Sustainability Team wanted to influence recycling beyond Kerr's processing facility and help employees with their own recycling needs.

SOLUTION

Kerr enrolled six employees in the Marion County Master Recycler program, an intensive, 60-hr process that trains individuals to reduce waste, conserve natural resources, motivate others to change their habits, and make a difference. The company encourages employees to take the class by paying their hourly wage for class time. There are currently three Master Recyclers on Kerr's Sustainability Team and three more working across the facility.

In 2014, Kerr established an on-site recycling center for employees who do not have curbside recycling at their homes and encourages them to use the center. The Master Recyclers are available as a resource to guide their coworkers in recycling properly. The company also hosts an annual "E-Recycling Event" where employees can bring their unwanted electrical items for recycling.

RESULTS

Kerr's practices have shown that it takes recycling very seriously and the Master Recyclers have broadened the company's thinking about recycling. The on-site recycling program has become such a success, that the Sustainability Team has expanded it to include styrofoam recycling, which is not collected curbside.

Donating Reusable Items Cuts Down on Waste and Helps the Community

Kerr Concentrates, Inc.

OPPORTUNITY

In its long-running effort to reuse and recycle its waste, Kerr Concentrates has implemented a number of programs to create value out of waste. Could some of these items be reused and provide benefits to the local community?.

SOLUTION

Kerr donates clean, used, plastic pails (from raw product delivered to the plant) to Marion County for use in its paint recycling program and to other non-profits. Marion County cleans, blends, and packages the paint in the pails and makes the recycled paint available for free to the public. Kerr also donates all of its refundable bottles and cans from the employee lunch room to Oregon

Green Schools. Kerr also encourages employees to bring their cans and bottles from home to contribute. In addition, the Sustainability Team plants and maintains a garden from which they donate the harvest to the community. The crops include: corn, beans, cucumbers, tomatoes, zucchini, peppers, and herbs.

RESULTS

Marion County's free paint program recycles and gives away up to 35,000 gallons of paint annually, and Kerr's donation saves the county approximately $36,000 annually in new material costs a year.

Energy Fairs Save Energy at Home and at Work

Darigold, Inc.

OPPORTUNITY

Darigold believes in the power of education. Teaching people ways to save energy at home not only saves them money but teaches them good habits that carry forward into the workplace. Darigold knows conserving energy is a team effort and wanted to get everyone involved in the education. Once people know how saving energy at home helps their pocketbooks they will become more interested in it becoming a part of their lives. As people become more energy aware at home, it then carries into the work place. Conserving energy is a team effort involving everybody.

SOLUTION

Once a year, each of Darigold's 11 plants holds an energy fair to promote and teach home energy conservation. Outside experts are invited to join and promote energy conservation with participation from local utilities, energy efficiency programs, and Darigold vendors. Each exhibitor or vendor is asked to make up an energy-related question about their product or service for employees to answer. Employees are encouraged to learn by visiting booths for energy tips and completing a quiz on topics covered, which is entered into a prize raffle at the end. Food is always provided and varies from sandwiches, barbeque, or a fully catered meal. Learning is encouraged in a fun and festive atmosphere with food and prizes. It is a voluntary event.

Energy fairs are accessible to workers and held at times to maximize participation during shift overlaps. Darigold Portland holds a daytime fair to span between day and swing shifts, and there are activities for the night crew also. Darigold Sunnyside goes even further by holding a fair during each shift (i.e., 11-2 for day shift, 8-10 for swing shift and even the next day for the night crew) with participation by the utilities and vendors at all three sessions.

Each plant puts their own twist on their energy fair to make it fun and interesting. For instance, Darigold Chehalis held an employee cook-off each of the last three years where employees compete for bragging rights. Chefs cook up their best recipe to each year's theme, such as chili the first year, salsa the second, and chicken wings in the third year. Ballots are collected with the top chef earning the annual title. Expanding interest and participation is a result, with greater number of entrants each of the last three years to compete for the prestigious title.

Another example to promote energy fairs to employees is at Darigold Rainer, which invited their local Tesla store to participate. Employees learned about electric cars and could also test drive a Tesla electric car by purchasing a ride ticket with all proceeds donated to a local charity.

RESULTS

The energy fairs have been successful at teaching employees energy savings at home. Many utilities offered free home assessments and audits. Some efficiency programs bring LED lightbulbs to change out during assessments. Employees are enthused to save money at home and bring that same knowledge with them to the workplace.

The Darigold energy fairs also teach employees about energy saving projects around the plant. A poster board and exhibits featuring the plant energy team's work is displayed at each year's energy fair. Posters typically include the plant energy team's charter, a list of completed projects and savings, and typically feature details on a recently completed energy savings project. These energy fairs provide each plant's energy team with a platform to share energy project successes and peer recognition of the energy team's accomplishments. Each Darigold plant has a cross-functional energy team that meets regularly for plant energy efficiency, some teams have separate committees to plan months in advance for the upcoming energy fair. Each Darigold plant goes through an annual energy program assessment, part of that assessment includes a score on that year's energy fairs.

Darigold has been successful educating its employees on energy savings. By creating exciting and interactive energy fairs, Darigold employees have learned to put energy savings practices in use at home and work.

Smart Commuter Helps Employees Reduce Their Carbon Footprints

Bellingham Cold Storage

OPPORTUNITY

Bellingham Cold Storage (BCS) continuously seeks ways to lower its environmental footprint. BCS saw an opportunity to encourage employees to reduce their own carbon footprints.

SOLUTION

BCS established the SMART Commuter Program, which incentivizes employees to find alternatives to single-occupancy vehicles in their commute to work. BCS added a commuter checkbox on the daily timesheet to make it easy for BCS employees to report their SMART trips and for the company to track the success of the program.

RESULTS

On any given day, over a third of BCS employees carpool, bike, bus, or walk to work.

SMART Commuter increased BCS's reputation as a great employer and as a company focused on sustainability. It was recognized by the Environmental Protection Agency as one of the "Best Workplaces for Commuters" and has twice won the State of Washington's Governor's Award for innovation in workplace commuting.

Corporate social responsibility practices improve employee commitment and level of engagement to their core job function and to the company.[1] Research suggests that involvement in the company's corporate responsibility practices teaches workers valuable new skills that they bring back to their regular roles in the company.

---

1 Jeanne Meister, "Corporate Social Responsibility: A Lever for Employee Attraction & Engagement," *Forbes*, June 7, 2012, http://www.forbes.com/sites/jeannemeister/2012/06/07/corporate-social-responsibility-a-lever-for-employee-attraction-engagement/.

Green Machine Program Encourages Employees to Use Alternative Transportation

Sierra Nevada Brewing Co.

OPPORTUNITY

Sierra Nevada Brewing Co. continuously looks for ways to lower the carbon imprint of the company and its employees. One way was to create an incentive program that would encourage and reward employees to use their bicycles as a form of transportation.

SOLUTION

Through Sierra Nevada's Green Machine program, employees who use a qualifying form of alternative transportation – biking, carpooling, skateboarding, walking, biodiesel or electric vehicles – at least three times per week get points through the company's incentivized health tracking program. Employees log in and track how many times they use qualifying transportation and can trade in their points for vouchers to local farmer's markets or enter to win fantastic prizes like Fit Bits.

Employees are also encouraged to take advantage of the Federal Bicycle Commuter Act benefit. This benefit provides an allowance of up to $20 per month to employees who ride their bikes to work at least more than half of their regularly scheduled shifts. The allowance can be used for reasonable expenses incurred in conjunction with riding to work, such as fixing the seat, breaks, light, bell, etc.

RESULTS

The Green Machine program has been highly successful since its inception in 2007, and participation continues to increase. There are more than 150 employees actively participating in the program and there are plans to increase that number with additional carpooling incentives at their North Carolina brewery.

PART TWO
ENVIRONMENTAL SUSTAINABILITY

Environmental Sustainability is availability of resources including water, land, and energy to grow and process food products at sustainable rates, quality, and cost through continuous improvement.

—Northwest Food Processors Sustainability Guide

INTRODUCING ENVIRONMENTAL SUSTAINABILITY

Food production practices can potentially have profound impacts on an ecosystem and its natural resources. The way we cultivate crops, redistribute water, and dispose of waste can mean the difference between a thriving wetlands and a desolate landscape. Through our raw products, food companies are directly linked to the natural environment. Responsible stewardship of the environment is critical to a sustained food industry.

Land provides the substance from which our food sources derive sustenance and grow. It is the foundation of the food industry. Unsustainable practices can lead to encroachment of invasive species, degradation of soil nutrients, and over-reliance on fertilizers and pesticides. The long-term viability of the food processing industry is dependent on healthy land resources.

Water is the lifeblood of the environment, providing a constant stream of sustenance that can enhance or limit a region's ability to survive. Water is a critical input to agriculture and food processing, and many of the larger food companies use over a million gallons of water per day. But water supply and availability are becoming significant concerns in parts of the Northwest as well as the nation. Industrial wastewater is also an important environmental concern. To assure that sufficient clean water is available for our and future generations, water must be efficiently used and wastewater properly treated and disposed.

Waste and Emissions are of particular concern as new food safety standards have demanded sanitary packaging and containers that when disposed of can present a significant burden to the environment. Today's foods are often individually wrapped, placed in lined retail packages, boxed for transport, and then placed on pallets or crates. This produces a substantial amount of solid waste that ends up in landfills and creates pollution.

Energy is needed to fuel farm equipment and run irrigation pumps, to run food processing and packaging equipment, and to transport goods to market. Food processing is an energy-intensive industry and is the second-largest industrial user of electricity in the Northwest. In addition, energy generation and fossil fuel use account for the vast majority of greenhouse gas emissions.

Questions to Ask

1. Does my company have policies and goals in place to manage our use of natural resources?
2. Does my company have reduction or efficiency goals for water, waste, and energy?
3. What types of waste does my company produce?
4. What are my suppliers doing to reduce waste or use resources more efficiently?
5. Can my company partner with nearby companies to reduce waste or increase efficiencies?

Automatic Flow Controls Save Water and Reduce Costs

Seneca Foods Corporation

OPPORTUNITY

The water supply for the flumes that convey product to processing equipment used to be manually regulated at Seneca Foods Corporation. Frequently, the flow to the flumes would exceed the flume capacity and water would spill onto the floor and down the drain. Seneca Foods spent time observing and measuring the overflow rate and determined that the wasted water averaged 36,000 gallons per day (25 gallons per minute).

SOLUTION

The water supply flow was automated by adding a float to control an Asco brand valve on the input line. This simple modification automatically controlled the flow to the amount of water necessary to keep the flumes operating efficiently with no wasted water.

RESULTS

The capital cost was approximately $1,500 to reduce water consumption and discharge by 1.8 million gallons per year during the 50-day operating period. Total savings on the combined cost of water supply and treatment was $6,842 per year.

Comprehensive Assessment and Plan Reduce Water Use by 24%

Lamb Weston

OPPORTUNITY

Lamb Weston sought to significantly reduce water use at one of its plants.

SOLUTION

The company conducted a comprehensive review of all plant water systems and piping and developed a cost-effective plan to reduce water use.

Plant teams from across the organization—engineers, area and team leads, managers, and maintenance personnel—were assigned to one or more of 28 areas within the plant. Each team identified water lines running through the plant, measured flow, and then verified and corrected existing piping drawings.

RESULTS

Collection of facility-wide water-use data led to the identification and implementation of 16 measures and 31 preventative maintenance items to reduce daily water use per pound of product by an average of 24%. In addition to implemented measures and items, the plant teams also identified further water use reduction opportunities.

Screen Solids and Use Low-Flow Spray Bars to Reduce Wastewater Costs

Del Monte Foods

OPPORTUNITY

Solids in the company's wastewater were high and extra fees were being paid to treat them. After reviewing options for removing the solids, Del Monte Foods determined that reducing the amounts of solids introduced into the water and improved screening would be the simplest options.

SOLUTION

A Lyco brand rotary screen was installed in the waste pit to screen solids out of the water prior to discharge. In addition, solid gutter plates were installed to help reduce the amount of large solids entering the wastewater stream and to make the screens work better.

While looking for ways to reduce water use, the company noticed that the water used in the preparation department could be reduced without affecting product quality. Water flow was reduced through installation of a filtered low-flow spray bar system throughout the preparation department. The filtration before the spray bar was important for preventing the spray nozzles from plugging.

RESULTS

This project reduced water consumption by 20,000 gallons per day as well as saving over $25,000 annually

Low Capital and Behavioral Changes Reduce Wastewater Discharges by 19%

Lamb Weston

OPPORTUNITY

A Lamb Weston vegetable plant sought to reduce its wastewater discharge.

SOLUTION

A thorough water-usage review helped the team identify conservation opportunities in several areas: Installing flow-restrictive devices and automatic-control valves for chill-system sprays, re-plumbing recycled process water for receiving wash water, and reducing freeze-tunnel defrost times as well as process water filter backwash cycles.

Further water savings measures included eliminating continual belt washing, chill room gutter-flushing, and the removal of a wash tank in carrot receiving.

Operating and maintenance personnel were engaged in sustaining the reductions through awareness education activities and daily use tracking.

RESULTS

The vegetable plant reduced wastewater discharge by 19% per pound of product during the six-month growing season via low-capital, high-awareness conservation efforts.

Rejuvenate Engineered Wetlands for More Effective Nutrient Recycling

Lamb Weston

OPPORTUNITY

Engineered wetlands were installed 17 years ago at this Lamb Weston location. The wetlands filter nutrient-dense wastewater prior to application on suitable land and crops. The company conducted the first major restoration of engineered wetlands at this location. This will ensure the continued protection of critical groundwater areas.

SOLUTION

Lamb Weston revitalized the process water treatment system to original design levels. The company restored five of the twelve wetland cells in its engineered water treatment system for this location. Restoration included removal of decaying plant vegetation, removal and recycling of sludge/debris from ponds, and transplanting vigorous cattails from other ponds.

RESULTS

In addition to more effective water-to-soil nutrient recycling, the wetland rejuvenation restored pond water flow and dispersion as well as open-water habitats.

Re-piping and Water Recycling Reduces Water Use and Energy Costs

Lamb Weston

OPPORTUNITY

Boiler operators are required to sample and monitor boiler water several times a day to assure its quality. When sampling, Lamb Weston operators noticed that a large amount of water was being wasted during the process. They wanted to develop a new system for more efficient water travel and for water recovery.

SOLUTION

Revise the piping system for sampling and allow the reuse of large volumes of reverse osmosis water.

RESULT

A 15% reduction in wasted water was realized. Another environmental and economic benefit was the reduction of heating inputs. The boiler water was recycled back to the storage tank at an already warm temperature, resulting in less energy needed to heat the water for the boiler.

Automatic Solenoid Valves Assure Water Used Only When Needed

The Dannon Company, Inc. (YoCream International)

OPPORTUNITY

YoCream manufactures frozen yogurt and frozen beverages for the foodservice industry. Containers are filled with yogurt using a machine on the production line called a carton filler. As cartons exit the filler, they are sprayed with a stream of water to ensure there is no yogurt on the outside of the carton. Historically, these spray nozzles had to be turned off manually at the end of the day or anytime there were no cartons going through the filler. During any technical downtime, the water continued to pour all over the conveyor belt and down the drain. YoCream wanted a way to ensure that water was sprayed only when cartons were going through the filler.

SOLUTION

Install solenoid valves with automation that turns the water on only if the carton infeed is engaged. This ensures the production line only uses water when needed. No extra sensors or equipment had to be installed other than the valves.

RESULTS

YoCream was able to save about 360 gallons of water per day.

Water Use Reduction and Wasted Product Recovery

Western Polymer Corporation

OPPORTUNITY

To produce modified potato starch for the paper industry, Western Polymer relies on groundwater from an aquifer that is overused and declining. The company desired to reduce its freshwater use and reliance on the aquifer.

SOLUTION

In 2002, the company started working to reduce fresh water usage by making changes to its starch cleaning system. In 2006, Western Polymer installed more water-efficient starch cleaning equipment that further reduced water usage. In early 2007, a recovery tank was added, allowing water to be recycled before it is released to land application.

RESULTS

Changes to the cleaning system have reduced both wastewater and solid waste discharges. Wastewater discharge was reduced 64% from 2002 to 2006, with a reduction of 88% for 2007. Solid waste (starch residue) was reduced 85% from 2005; the remaining 15% is now being used for agricultural feed.

Savings from the 619,650 to 729,000 pounds starch per year not discharged as waste has been over $100,000 per year from an investment of approximately $85,000. The changes also reduced the consumption and discharge of more than 290,400 pounds of cationic reagent with the wastewater and wasted starch. Freshwater consumption was reduced by 15,676,000 gallons in 2006 compared to 2002 and another 5,790,000 gallons in 2007, for a total reduction of 21,466,000 gallons per year.

Boiler Piping Improvements Reduce Water and Energy Consumption

Diana Naturals, Inc.

OPPORTUNITY

Diana Naturals uses steam from a boiler to extract moisture from its fruit and vegetable products to between a 1 and 5% ratio on the surface of their dryer drums. Heating approximately 9,200 gallons of water five to seven days a week, 24 hours a day, from 35 degrees to over 212 degrees to produce this steam used a lot of energy. The company wanted to implement enhancements to the boiler condensate system for the double drum dryers. Areas looked at for better energy efficiency included the amount of water being used to operate the boilers, the amount of water that was being discharged into the sanitary system, and also the cold temperature of the water supply.

SOLUTION

Diana Naturals partnered with its boiler chemical provider and boiler service company to develop a condensate return system with more energy-efficient plumbing, components, and boiler feed water control. Savings were realized by installing new piping and insulating lines and adding a modulating control value. A continuous loop system for the heated returned condensate now allows reuse of water.

RESULTS

This new system not only reduced water and energy use, but the consistent temperature allows better equipment performance for quicker processing, easier use of the dryers, and a more uniform temperature of the dehydrating surface for a more consistent finished product. The new system also reduced the amount of chemicals needed to maintain the boiler condition.

Bill Cummins, plant engineer, verified the efficiency of the new system by comparing 24- to 48-hour runs on identical products. Daily reports by plant maintenance personnel documented an 85% reduction in water use by the boiler. NW Natural Gas provided daily reports, via email, showing therms used per hour that indicated a 20% reduction in natural gas use. The return on investment, primarily from energy savings, boiler feed water consumption reduction, and reduced boiler chemical use, was seven months on a cost of $35,280.

Onsite Waste Water Treatment and Biogas Recovery Reduce Sewer Fees and Energy Costs

Sierra Nevada Brewing Co.

OPPORTUNITY

Brewery effluent water is typically very high in organic solids and requires more treatment than a typical residential effluent stream. As brewery production increased, so did Sierra Nevada Brewing Co.'s impact on the local municipal water treatment system.

SOLUTION

To reduce impact, the brewery installed an onsite wastewater treatment facility in 2002 to pretreat all of its brewing process water. Vaults around the brewery collect process water for treatment.

The water is screened to remove any solids like residual grain and hops which are sent to an onsite composter. An equalization tank ensures that the water is the appropriate temperature and pH. The water then moves into an anaerobic digester that produces methane-rich biogas. A recovery system captures this gas, cleans it up a bit, and sends it to Sierra Nevada's boilers to offset the natural gas needed to run the system. Following the anaerobic digestion phase, water is further treated in an aeration basin to remove biological compounds before finishing in clarifying basins to settle out remaining solids.

RESULTS

Sierra Nevada's treatment plant sends water roughly equivalent to residential effluent water composition to the municipal plant instead of water with a high solids content typical of a brewery. The treatment process eliminates roughly 90% of the loading in the water. Additionally, the biogas produced at the anaerobic digester can be burned in place of natural gas in the company's boilers. Sierra Nevada's water treatment system significantly reduces its impact on the municipal system, reduces sewer fees, and provides free fuel for its boilers. This project paid for itself in five years.

Reduced Water Use, Discharge and Solids Decrease Water Costs and Wastewater Fees

Quincy Foods, Inc.

OPPORTUNITY

Quincy Foods discharges wastewater to the City of Quincy Industrial Wastewater Treatment Plant (Quincy IWWTP). Discharge costs from the City are based 50% on flow and 50% on load in the water.

The Quincy Foods wastewater discharge was at or near the limit of 2.2 million gallons per day on a regular basis, and fees were high. In addition, the Quincy IWWTP was near its capacity and needed additional capacity for new industrial users. Reduced flows would save money, reduce water use, and help minimize future costs for expansion of the Quincy IWWTP, which would be shared by all dischargers.

SOLUTION

Quincy Foods staff made it a priority to reduce water use and created a two-phase project: Phase 1 would reduce water use and discharge volume and Phase 2 would reduce the load of biochemical oxygen demand (BOD) and total suspended solids (TSS). Phase 1 was implemented in steps:

Step 1: The most appropriate measurement for water use reduction was determined: gallons of water use per pound of finished product.

Step 2: All pipes, valves, and fittings were inspected, and leaks were identified and fixed.

Step 3: Better flow data was collected. Flow meters were placed on water supply lines to specific water use areas or equipment where possible, one line at a time. Hourly water use data was collected to correlate with processing activities.

Step 4: Data was reviewed, and associates got out on the floor to determine why and how the water use varied and what practices used the most water.

Step 5: Solutions and ideas for controlling water use and reusing water were tested and implemented:

- Fixed water leaks.
- Put spray nozzles with automatic shutoffs on open hoses.
- Revised cleaning practices to use less water by using foam and brushes to first loosen grime and debris and

then lightly hose off, instead of cleaning everything with high-pressure water.
- Reduced or eliminated the use of high-pressure water.
- Installed a screen to clean post-blancher chiller water and reused the chiller water to supplement the pre-blanch wash water.
- Revised blancher operations to reduce operating water levels and overflows to the minimum needed to maintain adequate quality with minimum water use.

In implementing the project, it was important to narrow down the project to workable steps to help determine the where, how, why, and what of changing water use. A majority of the effort was educational. Antiquated practices and habits required effort to retrain experienced operators into a new way of thinking. Changes to the practices required experimentation and testing to find out how much water reduction was appropriate and how much was too much.

RESULTS

Water use was reduced by half from 1.5 to 2 gallons of water per pound of product to 0.8 to 0.9 gallons per pound of product. The investment in Phase 1 entailed flow meters, automatic shut-off spray nozzles, repairs to leaks, a screen with tank, new piping for chiller water reuse, and employee training. The investment was minimal, and the return on the investment came as reduced water supply cost and reduced wastewater fees. In addition, energy costs were substantially reduced by improved blancher operations because less water was required to be heated and reduced water pressure was needed for cleanup.

The benefits of reduced water use are community-wide. The reduction in flow by Quincy Foods and the other local major food processor has allowed the Quincy IWWTP to accept cooling water from the local computer data center users who were discharging to the municipal wastewater treatment plant. The municipal wastewater treatment plant improved without the "clean" cooling water diluting its treatment, and the result is more reliable treatment to high-quality reclaimed wastewater for groundwater recharge. The reduced water use and groundwater recharge helps improve the long-term sustainability of the local groundwater aquifer, which has been declining.

Sustainable Farming Practices, Solar Power, Recycling and Rail

Wm. Bolthouse Farms, Inc., a Campbell Soup company

OPPORTUNITY

Farming has evolved over the years into a very large business. The inputs into the farm can be quite expensive and can result in higher cost for the grower as well as the consumer. Bolthouse Farms determined that there was ample opportunity to reduce use of fossil fuels and conserve inputs such as water and pesticides to the farms.

SOLUTION

Solutions implemented by Bolthouse Farms included:

- Solar power farming—use of solar panels to generate energy

- Pivot irrigation
- Geographical Information System (GIS) precision farming
- Soil depletion prevention
- Spray Safe pesticide program
- Fresh Logistics rail freight forwarding
- Recyclable packaging

RESULTS

- Solar power farming reduced emissions and fossil fuel use.
- Solar panels generate energy for powering the pumps used to water the fields and the motors used in pivot irrigation.
- Pivot irrigation results in 20% less water used than in previous irrigation methods.
- Pivot irrigation reduces the use of pipe tractors, which lowers fuel use and emissions.
- Precision farming, which implements the use of a Geographic Information System (GIS), improves agricultural output while reducing the use of natural resources, thus reducing the farming "footprint" on the land.
- Soil depletion prevention, which is accomplished using harvesters that reduce the amount of dirt hauled into the plant by 3–5%, thereby reducing soil depletion.
- The Spray Safe program reduces pesticide usage and prevents pesticide drift incidents, which can harm nearby people and crops.
- Fresh Logistics distributes fresh produce via high-speed rail from Bakersfield to Chicago. It's a cleaner distribution

model that reduces CO2 emissions by millions of pounds and diesel fuel by hundreds of gallons.
- Beverage and salad dressing containers use PET #1 recyclable, a portion of which is made with regrind plastic. Carrot bag film is LDPE #4 recyclable. This reduces landfill waste.

Bioswales Remove Pollution from Surface Water Runoff

New Seasons Market

OPPORTUNITY

New Seasons was well into the development of its fifth store when a representative of the local neighborhood association approached it with an environmental concern—storm water runoff. Besides polluting rivers and streams, runoff after rain causes flooding and erosion, destroying habitats and contributing to sewer overflows.

At the time, plans for the new store included 15,000 square feet of non-permeable surfaces, which would mean another million gallons of storm water flowing out into the Willamette River. The company learned that Portland's Environmental Services had grant money available for businesses interested in implementing stormwater controls. By creating bioswales (bioswales are landscape elements designed to help remove silt and pollution from surface runoff water), New Seasons could reduce the impact the building would have on the environment.

SOLUTION

Although the project was already well underway and making modifications would likely increase costs and cause a delay in opening the new store, New Seasons decided to add a bioswale to its plans. The process included:

- Amending and obtaining approval for revised architectural plans
- Applying for new permits
- Applying for the grant to offset the costs

Much to New Seasons' surprise, once common ground was established among all the entities, things began to happen quickly. New plans were drawn up and submitted, the city granted New Seasons $50,000 for the bioswale, and the permits were hand carried by city employees between departments to speed up the process. The new store—with a bioswale—opened on time.

RESULTS

Today New Seasons has bioswales at seven of its twelve stores, which cycle over four million gallons of rainwater annually. The company benefits by reducing its environmental impact and an increased reputation as a sustainable business.

For more information, read *Growing Local Value: How to Build Business Partnerships That Strengthen Your Community* by Laury Hammel and Gun Denhart.

Composting and Recycle Sorting Reduce Waste and Disposal Costs

Standing Stone Brewing Company

OPPORTUNITY

Standing Stone Brewing Company has always encouraged employees to share their ideas and suggestions. Adopting green practices in more recent years has given Standing Stone the opportunity to engage its employees in new and previously unforeseen ways.

A server in the on-site restaurant observed the company's day-to-day operations and saw opportunities to reduce Standing Stone's overall waste.

SOLUTION

The employee proposed new practices, including composting and recycle sorting, to reduce overall waste and environmental impacts.

RESULTS

A year after these low-cost practices were adopted, overall waste has decreased by 95%, reducing the company's waste removal expenses by $2,400 annually.

Recycling and Recovery Reduce Waste Disposal Fees and Generate Revenue

Sierra Nevada Brewing Co.

OPPORTUNITY

Waste disposal fees are typically seen as a necessity for a business and something that cannot be avoided. However, what many fail to realize is that the materials that are being thrown away are resources that should and need to be recovered for beneficial reuse and recycling and can often bring in a source of revenue.

SOLUTION

Sierra Nevada Brewing Co. has established a world-class recycling and resource recovery program to keep materials from ending up in a landfill. Cardboard, shrink-wrap, cans, bottles, glass, scrap metal, paper, batteries, light bulbs, used motor oil, and food scraps are just some of the materials that are sorted out of the trash and recycled.

RESULTS

Through creative programs and partnerships, Sierra Nevada successfully diverts 99.8% of its total solid waste from landfill – sending only 0.2% of the entire facility's total discards to a landfill.

Recycling programs are inexpensive to establish, returns are often almost immediate, and a revenue stream can be realized. Spent grain makes up the bulk of the material leaving the brewery and can be sold as a protein rich feed for livestock. Because it's such a specialized byproduct, if it is removed from the diversion equation, Sierra Nevada realizes an average of $275,000 annual savings simply by recycling things like cardboard, shrink wrap, metal, and plastics and composting food scraps. There are also significant greenhouse gas emission reductions associated with recycling as well as reduced energy and water consumption when manufacturing with recycled materials instead of virgin materials.

Reusable and Returnable Bags Reduce Paper Waste

Western Polymer Corporation

OPPORTUNITY

Western Polymer Corporation recovers starch from French fry and potato chip processing water before it enters the waste stream and modifies it for use in the paper industry.

The company originally packaged its starch products in 50-pound paper bags. All paper bags became waste at Western Polymer's plant or at its customers' locations and the company wanted a way to reduce this waste.

SOLUTION

To reduce the amount of waste paper, Western Polymer implemented the use of reusable, returnable bulk bags rather than disposable paper bags. Over the course of 15 years, the company was able to switch most customers to reusable bulk bags. The bulk bags are returned to Western Polymer and reused multiple times. When worn out, they are shipped to a recycler, completely avoiding landfill disposal.

RESULTS

This program has eliminated 364,000 pounds of paper waste per year.

In addition, the company added mechanical handling equipment to enable hydrated lime for the starch manufacturing process to be delivered and utilized with reusable bulk bags rather than 50-pound paper bags. This change eliminated 8,750 pounds of paper waste per year and reduced employees' exposure to hydrated lime by not having to physically handle the 50-pound paper bags.

Composing Reduces Waste and Landfill Costs

New Seasons Market

OPPORTUNITY

Since its founding in 2000, New Seasons Market has been committed to sustainable practices. In 2003, the company began separating organics for composting at all of its stores. New Seasons knew it could do more, so it enlisted the help of Portland Composts!, a Portland Bureau of Planning and Sustainability Initiative, in 2007.

SOLUTION

The program that was developed is called "Waste to Worth" and has three main components:

- Each of the 12 New Seasons stores targets the departments with the most waste.

- Color-coded containers—consistent across stores—are placed at points of high waste generation.
- Customized signage and training materials match both the waste guidance materials and the company's branding.

RESULTS

Every New Seasons store recycles and composts, resulting in a 50% reduction in overall garbage and conversion of 2,140 tons of organic waste to compost annually. Overall, composting saves New Seasons Market 30% compared to landfill costs, which amounted to more than $25,000 in 2011.

HotRot Composter Reduces Organic Waste and Produces Soil Amendments for Agricultural Application

Sierra Nevada Brewing Company

OPPORTUNITY

When organics are sent to a landfill instead of being composted, they produce methane as they break down. Methane is roughly 21 times more potent as a greenhouse gas than carbon dioxide, and food scraps in landfills are a primary source of methane. Chico, California, is located at the northern end of the Sacramento Valley and is in a fairly rural community. There are minimal composting outlets for the communities in the region and no food scrap composting options.

SOLUTION

Sierra Nevada Brewing Co. encouraged the local community to pursue a regional food scraps composting facility for four years. When encouragement resulted in no action, Sierra Nevada decided to purchase its own composting system. In September 2010, Sierra Nevada installed the country's first HotRot composting system to handle all of the brewery's spent food scraps and some spent brewing ingredients. The HotRot is capable of composting 5,000 pounds of organic material daily and produces a stable, nutrient-rich soil amendment that is used in onsite agricultural activities.

RESULTS

The brewery is composting all food scraps from its restaurant, concert venue, and break rooms (pre- and post-consumer), paper towels, hops from its dry hopping process, spent grain that is screened out of the wastewater effluent stream, and miscellaneous landscaping debris.

The HotRot composting system exemplifies an excellent closed-loop system where discards from the restaurant are turned into compost, which is used on the field that grows produce for the restaurant, which then creates the scraps that go right back out to the field.

Benefits from the system include reduced waste disposal fees, reduced greenhouse gas emissions, nutrient-rich soil amendment for use in onsite agricultural activities, opportunities to educate employees and consumers on important waste diversion practices, and a great story to tell. While the system has a long payback – close to 15 years – Sierra Nevada is now 5 years ahead of the curve now that the state of California has implemented a ban on organics going to landfills while other local generators affected by the legislation takin effect in April 2016 are scrambling to find a solution.

Rail Transfer Facility Allows Greater Use of More Efficient and Cleaner Rail Transportation

Sierra Nevada Brewing Company

OPPORTUNITY

Transportation has arguably the most damaging environmental impacts in all of Sierra Nevada Brewing Company's operations, but it is something that is required in order for the company to sell its beers. Sierra Nevada recognizes that it will not entirely escape the negative impacts of transportation, but also knows that there are some very important things the company can do to reduce those impacts.

SOLUTION

In 2009, Sierra Nevada completed construction of a malt transfer facility just two miles from its Chico brewery. The facility includes more than two miles of rail track that come off of the main rail line that runs through Chico, as well as equipment to transfer malted barley from rail cars and into truck trailers.

Sierra Nevada is also shipping finished product via intermodal transportation. Intermodal transportation means that a truck trailer is filled with product at the brewery and driven to the closest rail transfer facility. Trailers are loaded onto the train and railed across the United States instead of being trucked. More than 70% of shipments from Sierra Nevada's Chico brewery are arriving on the east coast via rail.

RESULTS

Rail is an incredibly efficient and cost-effective way to move materials. Sierra Nevada now receives approximately 95% of its malt through the transfer facility. There are between three to four truckloads of malt in one rail car and multiple rail cars on each train, increasing the efficiency. Rail is 50% cleaner than traditional over-the-road truck travel. Benefits include reduced cost, increased efficiency, reduced fossil fuel use, and reduced greenhouse gas emissions. Sierra Nevada spent more than $1 million on the transfer facility, but it paid for itself in less than two years.

Sonic Air Dryers More Energy Efficient than Compressed Air Dryers

Seneca Foods Corporation

OPPORTUNITY

Compressed air was used to remove water from cans on the production line before can coders marked the cans with numbers and text. This required energy to produce and maintain air pressure.

SOLUTION

The company replaced compressed air dryers with sonic air dryers. Sonic air dryers can perform the same water removal function but eliminate the need for high-energy use compressed air dryers. Seneca Foods Corporation had prior success with sonic dryers in the same application and had several sonic dryers left over from previous conversions in other areas.

RESULTS

The replacement saved the difference in cost between running the sonic dryers and operating the compressed air dryers. Eliminating the continuous use of compressed air through a ¼-inch airline reduced electrical energy consumption by 186,000 kilowatt-hours (kWh) per year at a cost savings of $9,300 per year.

Energy Efficiency Results in Stable Energy Costs Even with Increased Production

Sierra Nevada Brewing Co.

OPPORTUNITY

One can generate all the green power in the world one wants to, but if that power is not used efficiently, the purpose has been defeated. This rings true at Sierra Nevada Brewing Co., and the company has taken numerous steps to increase the energy efficiency of not only its equipment but of processes and employee behavior.

SOLUTION

Sierra Nevada has implemented the following energy efficiency measures:

- Tracking of electricity consumption
    - Tracking allows the user to notice and react quicker if there is something wrong in the process that is using more energy than it should. It also allows for the identification of positive trends in order to make sure they are continued.
- Retrofit of lighting fixtures and control systems
- Automation of equipment and processes
- Variable frequency drives on motors and pumps
- Increased water conservation
    - Water use, especially at a brewery, requires ample energy to move, treat, and use. When water is conserved, the energy that goes into its use is also conserved.

RESULTS

Sierra Nevada has been able to drive its kWh per barrel intensity down consistently over the last five years, resulting in stable energy costs despite the fact that production has increased. Some projects are more cost-intensive than others, but most do not involve a cost at all, simply a change in the way something is done. Since 2008, Sierra Nevada has reduced energy intensity per barrel of beer produced by 21%

Lighting Retrofit of Old System Reduces Energy Costs

Del Monte Foods

OPPORTUNITY

Del Monte Foods continuously seeks ways to reduce cost and energy consumption. Looking for ways to reduce energy use, the Yakima plant team determined that the best option was to reduce energy consumption in the old, outdated lighting system.

SOLUTION

The team proposed a lighting retrofit project to replace 100% of internal plant lighting with modern T8 fixtures and lamps. In order to pay for the $140,000 project, the Yakima team applied for two grants, which provided a total of $88,000 to the plant to help fund this project, reducing Del Monte's total cost for this project to $52,000.

RESULTS

The ongoing annual savings of 538,000 kWh produces cost savings of $25,000 per year for a return on investment in just over two years including the grant (and less than six years if the grant isn't considered).

Solar Power Reduces Demand Charges and Supplies Part of Power Needs

Sierra Nevada Brewing Co.

OPPORTUNITY

Sierra Nevada Brewing Co. relies on the local power grid for electricity and a large portion of the monthly utility bill includes demand charges. Demand charges are based on the highest level of electricity a customer draws during specific times of the day with peak use being the most expensive and occurring from noon-6:00pm, Monday-Friday.

SOLUTION

In 2010, Sierra Nevada Brewing Co. completed installation of a 2 megawatt solar system and is now one of the largest privately owned solar installations in the country. Solar photovoltaic electricity is a clean and 100% renewable source of electricity. Sierra Nevada's solar system covers a three-acre parking lot as well as all available roof space. Sierra Nevada's onsite daycare facility and rail facility are also 100% solar powered.

RESULTS

Altogether, Sierra Nevada's solar systems are capable of producing 2 megawatts of direct current (DC) electricity and include over 10,500 individual photovoltaic panels. In 2014, the solar system produced 2,646,383 kWh, or 19.5% of Sierra Nevada's total electricity needs—roughly equivalent to powering 265 average American households. Solar panels are ideal for utility customers that are on a time-of-use rate structure because solar panels perform during the peak of the day when electricity is the most expensive. If Sierra Nevada would have purchased the electricity their solar system provided, they would have spent more than $350,000 just for the electricity, not factoring in any demand charges. Demand charges are reduced by roughly $150,000 per year as a result of the solar panels operations.

Solar panels will obviously reduce a company's utility costs, but there are a number of other peripheral benefits to utilizing solar. Investing in alternative energy ensures a more stable source of power for future years, demonstrates corporate citizenship and environmental stewardship, reduces the company environmental footprint, and builds a culture that employees are happy to be a part of.

Sierra Nevada spent roughly $2 million out-of-pocket for the solar systems. This was after the many state and federal rebates and incentives the company received for installing the system and the system is expected to pay for itself in the next two years. For more information, see http://www.sierranevada.com/brewery/about-us/sustainability.

Energy Efficient Air Compressor Project Produces Significant Energy Savings

Seneca Foods Corporation

OPPORTUNITY

A Seneca Foods Corporation facility had an antiquated, poorly working air system that ran a can dryer.

The company engaged its local equipment maintenance vendor to analyze the air system and identify options to improve operating efficiency.

SOLUTION

Efficiency improvements included installing one new compressor with a variable frequency drive and a new dryer. The company also installed a new 5,000-gallon air holding tank to help handle the demand surges from the retorts (sterilization process).

RESULTS

The total cost of the project was approximately $100,000, but energy conservation incentives from the electrical utility would offset some of the cost once the savings were verified. Overall, after verification by the equipment maintenance vendor, the improvements to the air system reduced the facility's energy consumption by 440,000 kilowatt-hours per year. The electric utility company issued incentives of approximately $53,000, bringing the net capital cost to $47,000. Seneca Foods saves $22,000 per year in electricity costs and now has updated equipment that works.

Tracking and Analyzing Water Use Reveals Hidden Leaks

Lamb Weston

OPPORTUNITY

In September 2014, a team of employees at one of Lamb Weston's frozen potato facilities decided to tackle the issue of lost water in one of the processing lines. Tracking water use and loss is extremely difficult in enclosed systems, where overflow occurs out of sight. And, the cost of permanent flow meters can be prohibitive to multiple installations. The team did some out-of-the-box thinking to create a method to find lost water within their systems.

SOLUTION

Focusing on pump loops, where water is often out of sight, the team used a portable flow metering device to measure water flow when the fill valve was open for each pump loop. A controls technician then wrote a program to calculate and track water use based on the amount of time a fill valve was open. After analyzing the data, the team found that a hidden under-floor hole in a pipe was losing significant water each day, which would never have been found otherwise. The team also balanced several pump loops that were also losing water intermittently. Using this new program, the facility can now quickly spot a problem arising on any of its pump loops.

RESULTS

After correcting the identified leaks and balancing the remaining pump loops, this facility was able to realize a 3% reduction in water use. Employees were encouraged to problem-solve and be creative in finding solutions for assessing water loss—which enables them to keep their eyes open for other improvements and fixes.

Reducing kWh with a Fan VFD and Pump System Automation

Del Monte Foods

OPPORTUNITY

In 2012, Del Monte Foods' Toppenish, Washington facility partnered with Pacific Power and Cascade Energy to find energy saving projects throughout the plant. Two unrelated capital projects were quickly found that were immediately addressable— fan variable frequency drive and pump automation systems.

SOLUTION

A VFD was installed on the cooling tower fan so that the fan could be slowed down based on the temperature of the water. This saved energy by allowing for more flexible temperature control based on production conditions. The second project installed a pressure sensor on the three-pump Kobe system so that only the number of 100HP pumps needed at any given time will actually run.

RESULTS

Meeting corporate ROI expectations were difficult due to seasonal operation, but with the help of incentives through the utilities, plant managers decided to move forward with the projects. As a result of this project, the Toppenish facility was able to save an estimated 139,000 kWh annually. This equaled an annual savings of $7000.

Eliminating Negative Air Conveyance Saves Energy and Maintenance

Del Monte Foods

OPPORTUNITY

During the installation of a new Olney Flotation Corn Cleaner unit, the plant superintendent found a way to eliminate the negative air system in the manufacturing process. Negative air was being used to vacuum convey corn to a location that was difficult to accommodate belt conveyors. The negative air system used a lot of energy and also frequently became plugged with corn, causing downtime on the production line.

SOLUTION

By reconfiguring equipment, it was possible to use two small conveyors in place of the negative air conveyance. The team decided to remove the negative air conveyance because of the energy saving opportunity as well as the more sanitary design of the new conveyance. The team was able to eliminate a 40 HP vacuum pump and replace that with 2 HP worth of conveyance. The Negative Air Vacuum system had 80' of 3" tubing that was hard to clean and required additional water and chemicals, which are no longer required. The team used a CAD drawing equipment layout to ensure success of the final installation.

RESULTS

Meeting corporate ROI expectations were difficult due to seasonal operation, but the change to the production line made sense, so the team pushed forward. The Toppenish facility was able to save 39,000 kWh annually, which equated to about $2000/year. The new conveyance has proven very sanitary and easy to clean and there has been no downtime with the new system.

Heat Reclaim on Corn Processing Line Saves Energy

Del Monte Foods

OPPORTUNITY

In 2015, the Del Monte Engineering Department worked with the Washington State University Energy Extension Program to complete a project on the corn processing line that began in 2011. At that time, it was not feasible to change the Cream Style part of the heat reclaim project because of high equipment cost, so only the boiler and Whole Kernel heat reclaim was completed. After seeing the success of the first part of the project, the team moved forward with implementation across the processing line.

SOLUTION

The Cream Style Blend Tank was replaced and with heat reclaim. This enabled the old Cream Style Blend Tank to be used for hot water storage, which made the project affordable. The main components of the project were 200' of piping and several valves. Installation was done by plant personnel and contractors.

RESULTS

As a result of this project, the Toppenish facility was able to save an estimated 1532 MMBTU annually, which equates to annual savings of $7600.

Lighting Upgrades Produce Big Savings and Improved Visibility

Del Monte Foods

OPPORTUNITY

In 2011, Del Monte's Toppenish, Washington plant worked with Pacific Power and Cascade Energy to determine opportunities for a lighting upgrade. Not only were the bulbs of an older variety, but the fixtures needed to be replaced, too, which made this project a major capital investment, but an important one. Managers had determined that better lighting was needed for operation and safety of employees.

SOLUTION

This project consisted of replacing or retrofitting over 600 fixtures (old high intensity discharge) with newer T8 and T5 fluorescent technology. Plant electricians did the entire installation.

RESULTS

Electricity is only 5 cents per kWh in the Yakima Valley so the only way the project team was able to make this project pass the IRR hurdle without installing very low quality lighting fixtures was due to incentives of $47,000 from Pacific Power and a $48,000 grant from WSU Energy Program. The project saves a whopping 654,000 kWh and $37,000 every year. However, 50 lights in the warehouse were not included in this project because they were not accessible due to product stacks. Del Monte has not yet secured funding for these lights. Lesson learned: find a way to get it done all at one time.

Innovative Packaging Eliminates Crates and Allows Direct Palletizing

Darigold, Inc.

OPPORTUNITY

Most people are familiar with the common milk crate. These sturdy plastic crates are a staple for moving and basement storage, but cause headaches for dairy companies. A conventional one-gallon milk jug has to be placed into a plastic crate so that it can be handled and shipped. When the crates arrive at a retail location, the jugs are removed and placed into the cooler. The empty crates then have to be shipped back to the processing facility where they are inspected and washed. Needless to say, some crates get stolen, others break over time and need to be replaced. Some retailers do not return these crates to dairy companies, causing a proliferation of plastic products and wasted resources.

SOLUTION

In 2008, Darigold's Seattle plant began packaging its milk in rectangular-shaped jugs. This innovative packaging eliminates the need for any milk crates because the jugs can be directly palletized.

RESULTS

"Caseless" milk jugs have saved Darigold a tremendous amount of time and money. The company does not have to continuously order crates, transport them to and from retailers, or use the water and chemicals needed to wash used crates. The new jugs have changed the process of moving milk from the plant to customers, reducing touch points from 23 to 8. This story shows that thinking outside the crate has its benefits!

Eliminating Chemicals and Reducing Blowdown in Cooling Tower Maintenance

G & G Orchards, Inc. and HydroFLOW USA.

OPPORTUNITY

The cooling tower at G&G Orchards required the use of chemicals to counteract the limescale accumulation as well as algae slime. The limescale was making the cooling tower less efficient and wasting water due to excessive blowdowns. This process, which flushes a portion of high mineral concentration cooling tower system water down the drain, while simultaneously replacing it with fresh water, wastes water and flushes chemicals into the environment. Prior to the installation of the HydroFLOW unit, the owner was having issues with his condensers becoming very thick with slime and his evaporator was full of algae. Chemical treatment did not fix the problem and G & G Orchards estimated that it was using $3,000 worth of chemicals each month.

SOLUTION

Install a HydroFLOW unit to remove existing limescale deposits, prevent limescale accumulation and eliminate the need for chemicals. However, the owner of G&G Orchards was skeptical about the ability of the unit to perform its stated abilities, so the supplier offered to implement a two-month trial with the HydroFLOW unit, at no charge, to prove that the technology was better than using chemicals.

RESULTS

After two months of use with no chemical application, G & G Orchards was happy to see real results. Through a visual inspection, there were no algae blooms and the bare metal on the cooling tower was beginning to show. Blow down was also reduced by 50%. Because the HydroFLOW unit does not use any chemicals to condition the water, G & G Orchards eliminated use of chemicals. The chemicals used to combat scale and bio in the cooling towers can be quite caustic. When the towers scale up, employees must enter the towers to clean them. If they inhale the chemicals or get them in their eyes or on their skin, it can be quite irritating and unhealthy. The discontinued use of chemicals in the cooling towers allows for a safer work environment and also helps keep the orchard environmentally friendly.

G & G Orchards no longer pays $3000/month in chemicals costs. Total return on investment was 18 months.

Interview with Renee Garcia, the owner of G & G Orchards - http://bit.ly/1UsWbMI.

Technology Reduces Scale on Apples and Increases Profits

Allan Brothers, Inc. and HydroFLOW USA.

OPPORTUNITY

Allan Brothers grows apples throughout Eastern Washington. Their orchards incorporate overhead sprayers for temperature control and sun damage protection. The water used at several of Allan Brothers' orchards in Eastern Washington is "hard" – containing high levels of calcium, magnesium, and manganese. The water is treated with acid to combat the lime scale deposits that would clog the sprayers and coat the apples. Scale staining can reduce the grade rating of the apples and reduce the grower's earning potential. In addition, the use of the chemicals to combat the scale is costly and not always environmentally-friendly.

SOLUTION

Install a HydroFLOW unit on the pipe that supplies water to the orchard to eliminate scale. Allan Brothers was skeptical as they had tried other devices that did not work. To prove the technology, the HydroFLOW team worked with orchard operators to set up a test site during the off season by hanging apples (from cold storage) from cherry trees. They used the standard sprayers on one set (the control group) and HydroFLOW-treated water on another set (the experimental group). Both groups were watered as they normally would have been during the growing season.

RESULTS

The control group continued to develop hard scale, which was nearly impossible to remove. The experimental group sprayed with the HydroFLOW treated water had only a 5% rejection rate. Any scale on these apples had been reduced to a fine powder and was easily washed off without chemicals. The apples that were watered without the HydroFLOW treated water still had a 50% rejection rate. The benefits were obvious.

Allan Brothers was able to shift away from the use of acid and other chemicals, which alone contributed to an ROI of less than one year. Surprisingly, the HydroFLOW unit placed on the water reservoir pipe ended up clearing the pond of algae, which eliminated the need to empty and clean the reservoir every time the algae clogged the pipes. Furthermore, the employees no longer had to work with hazardous chemicals, which reduces the risk of injury and workers' compensation claims. And most importantly, the apples were able to be sold at the highest rating, which earned growers higher margins.

Diverting Waste Saves Money and Reduces Environmental Impacts

Kerr Concentrates, Inc.

OPPORTUNITY

Juice concentrate production produces millions of pounds of organic waste every year. The processing equipment extracts fruit juices and purees, and a company like Salem's Kerr Concentrates is left with large amounts of solid organic waste. Along with the solids, Kerr's production line produces thousands of gallons of liquid from micro filtration processes. Prior to 2010, Kerr was sending its solid waste to a farm for cattle feed, but this was expensive to haul. In addition, the biochemical oxygen demand (BOD) and solids in its wastewater was too high for the municipal wastewater system. Something needed to be done.

SOLUTION

In 2010, Kerr began shipping its solid waste and wastewater from the micro filter to a local bio-generating facility. The facility takes almost 100 tons of solid organic waste from its farms and food industry partners every day. An anaerobic digester produces methane to power an engine that generates electricity and feeds it back to the grid. After the gas is harvested, the leftover sludge is used as fertilizer. In 2016, Kerr began sending its solid waste and solids from the micro filter to a 3rd party composting company.

RESULTS

Annually, Kerr prevents over 8 million pounds of organic waste and over 100,000 gallons of organic liquid from entering the waste stream – about 95% of its organic waste. Kerr also became certified by Marion County's EarthWISE program and in recognition of its outstanding sustainability efforts received the Mid-Willamette Valley Green Award as 2015 EarthWISE Business of the Year.

Lighting Replacements and Strategic Energy Management Deliver Significant Energy Savings

Kerr Concentrates, Inc.

OPPORTUNITY

Kerr Concentrates began working with Energy Trust of Oregon (ETO) in 2014 to assess the lighting in its facility and determine how to transition to more efficient, brighter and cleaner lighting systems. Kerr was also interested in other energy savings opportunities as well.

SOLUTION

The Sustainably Team, with knowledge gained from NWFPA and other partners, took it upon themselves to update lighting in the facility. Phase I of the project included replacing metal halide, high pressure sodium and fluorescent fixtures throughout the plant and the outside grounds with LED lighting with motion and photovoltaic sensors. By 2016, the team completed Phase II, which included all the office and lab area lighting.

Four members of Kerr's Sustainability Team worked with ETO and enrolled in its Strategic Energy Management (SEM) program. This year-long process uncovered numerous energy savings opportunities. In 2016, the team began working with Every Watt Matters to discover more energy efficiency measures. These included replacing its metal halide, high pressure sodium, and fluorescent fixtures throughout the plant and outside grounds to LED lighting with motion and photovoltaic sensors.

RESULTS

Replacing old lighting fixtures with LEDs changed the tone and feel of the facility. Phase I produced energy savings of 287,000 kWh per year and annual carbon dioxide reductions of 320,000 metric tons. Phase II saved another 182,000 kWh per year. The ETO SEM Program's energy savings totaled 198,500 kWh per year. The Team has committed to ETO's SEM Continuous Improvement year-long program in fall 2016, which will produce further energy savings. Total kWh saved through Phase I and II and the SEM Program totaled 655,932 kWh annually.

Eliminating Redundant Uses Saves Water

Kerr Concentrates, Inc.

OPPORTUNITY

Kerr's Sustainability Team challenged itself to go out into the facility and find places for water efficiency improvements. One team member spoke with an operator who noticed a redundancy in pre-rinse cycles (4 – 5 cycles) for the finished juice tanks, which may not have been necessary. This process also caused lengthy downtime while employees waited for the rinse cycles to be completed.

SOLUTION

The operator worked with the Kerr's contracted sanitation provider to run tests and modify the cleaning program. They reduced cleaning cycle times on two of the finished juice tanks resulting in a reduction of 12 minutes of cleaning time per tank cycle. The

Sustainability Team also found savings with a closed loop water flush system for the mechanical seals that cool production pumps.

RESULTS

The changes in the cleaning process produced 1,765 gallons of water saved per tank cleaning. This results in an annual reduction of water use of approximately 550,000 gallons, which is no longer discharged to the city system. The closed loop water flush system resulted in an annual reduction of use and discharge of 332,000 gallons of water.

Partnerships to Repurpose Waxed Cardboard

New Seasons Market

OPPORTUNITY

In March 2015, Metro, the regional government in the Portland, OR area, changed its rules for business composting. It would no longer accept "compostable" cups, utensils, to-go containers, or waxed cardboard boxes that were ubiquitous in the area's grocery stores, restaurants, and food distributors. Understanding that this meant these materials were destined for the landfill, New Seasons Market's sustainability team stepped up to make sure the cardboard would not end up in the landfill.

SOLUTION

The team partnered with California-based CleanFlame, the makers of a widely-available, ultra-clean-burning recycled fuel log. CleanFlame could use the waxed cardboard to make pressed logs that would replace the need to harvest trees for firewood.

However, CleanFlame would only take the cardboard if it could fill a semi-trailer truck on the truck's return trip back to California (thus reducing the waste of an empty truck). New Seasons partnered with other area grocery stores to supply enough waxed cardboard to fill the trucks. The amount of diverted cardboard filled CleanFlame's stock requirements, so New Seasons began working with IWS, a company out of Georgia that repurposes such material.

RESULTS

The partnership helped divert and recycle over 200 tons of waxed cardboard in 2015. New Seasons saves $120,000 annually by avoiding the cost of sending this cardboard to the landfill.

Consolidating Vendors' Shipments Reduces Number of Deliveries and Greenhouse Gas Emissions

New Seasons Market and B-Line Sustainable Urban Delivery

OPPORTUNITY

In August 2013, New Seasons Market launched a program called Local Finds to secure products from very small, hyper-local vendors for its shelves. As of early 2015, New Seasons carried 137 vendors that were discovered through the Local Finds program. While the program was a success, management noticed the huge increase in deliveries to each of its stores— sometimes over 80 per day. A large number of these were Local Finds vendors, which were driving their personal cars through the dense urban core to deliver product to New Seasons stores throughout Portland. Oregon.

SOLUTION

New Seasons partnered with B-Line Sustainable Urban Delivery to consolidate distribution and transport of Local Finds products to its stores. B-Line uses electric-assist cargo trikes to deliver a variety of products across Portland. New Seasons management worked with Local Finds vendors to encourage consolidation with B-Line and supported B-Line's distribution expansion, which includes a refrigerated warehouse in Portland's Central Eastside district.

RESULTS

In just one year, 25 small businesses were participating in the program, with more in the works. As of April 2015, this program has saved 1105 individual distribution trips by Local Finds vendors to New Seasons Markets and reduced associated CO_2 emissions by 15,000 lbs. B-Line has moved into the new distribution space and is increasing its fleet of trikes, while partnering with more businesses to decrease congestion on the roads, air pollution, and wear on the city's infrastructure.

Successful Implementation of Process Wastewater Recycling

J.R. Simplot Company

OPPORTUNITY

A state of the art potato processing facility was constructed to replace the production capacity of three aging processing plants. A significant challenge for the new facility was the need to triple factory production while utilizing an existing land application system that previously served the wastewater management needs for a much smaller processing plant. Implementing a high level of production plant water use efficiency and innovative wastewater treatment were essential to project success.

SOLUTION

In order to address the wastewater challenges presented by the new potato processing facility, Simplot established the following sustainability goals for designing the wastewater treatment system.

1. New facility must use 50% less freshwater than the three older processing facilities that were being replaced by the new facility. Using less freshwater at the processing plant was critical to ensure the facility could continue to operate during winter months without exceeding process water storage pond limits.
2. Achieve a high quality of wastewater treatment to manage increased loading rates of COD, nitrogen, and phosphorus associated with increased production from the processing plant. Higher level of wastewater treatment was necessary to ensure the facility met permitted limits for managing nutrients within the land application system.
3. Return treated process water back to the potato production facility for reuse. Following wastewater treatment, a portion of the total flow would undergo advanced treatment and disinfection to achieve a water quality equivalent to drinking water. This water would be returned to the processing plant to reduce the demand for freshwater and reduce the amount sent to the land application system.

Following the above sustainability goals, the integrated design team constructed and commissioned a complex and innovative process water treatment and return plant (PWTRP) as shown below.

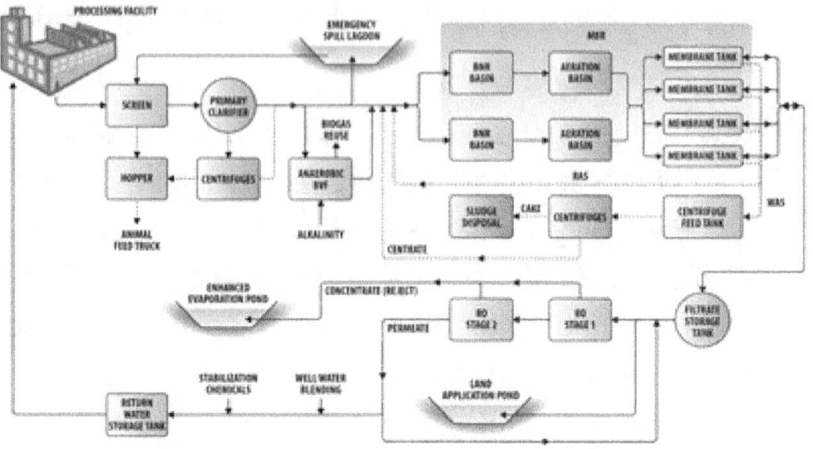

Key components of the PWTRP included:

- Anaerobic digestion
- Biological nutrient removal
- MBR system (Ultra Filtration)
- 2 stage reverse osmosis with active evaporation of RO reject stream

Once constructed the PWTRP system provided operators the flexibility to significantly reduce wastewater strength and return a significant portion of treated process water to be reused in the production facility.

RESULTS

- Following startup of the new potato processing facility, a 46% reduction in freshwater use was observed compared to the average combined water use of the three older facilities. This equates to about 52 million gallons saved per month.
- Using biological and advanced filtration, the project achieved treatment efficiencies of 99% COD and

Ammonia, and 87% of phosphorus to comfortably meet the land application permit requirements.
- Using reverse osmosis and disinfection, a significant portion of process wastewater can reliably meet drinking water standards. This water is recirculated into the plant to reduce fresh water demand. Up to 75% of the facility wastewater flow can be recovered.

Engaging Industrial Partners to Support Composting of Organic Waste Byproducts

J.R. Simplot Company

OPPORTUNITY

The process of producing frozen french fries from raw potatoes generates a significant amount of potato waste and organic byproducts (soils, vegetation, vines, etc.). It is a common industry practice for organic waste byproducts to be applied to agricultural lands, sent to landfill or utilized by livestock feeding operations. For Simplot Canada, dealing with organic waste byproducts involved a complex and resource intense waste management system involving multiple contractors, land owners, and a small fleet of heavy duty equipment. For these reasons, it was felt that a more sustainable, less resource-intensive solution was necessary to manage organic waste byproducts. Industrial scale composting presented an opportunity that met the goals of the project. The one problem is that an industrial scale composting facility did not exist near the processing facility. The challenge for this project was to engage a third party contractor to provide industrial composting services where none currently existed. Another challenge was to convince regulatory agencies that composting byproducts was a viable solution for managing industrial organic wastes in a cold weather climate.

SOLUTION

The first step was to engage a regional composting contractor to determine interest in providing industrial composting services in close proximity to the processing plant. In order to demonstrate to the contractor and regulators that the project would be successful, the processing facility sponsored a small scale pilot composting project. During the pilot project regular samples and records were maintained to demonstrate the effectiveness of industrial composting in a cold weather climate. Successful composting requires the correct balance of organic materials. During the pilot project it was found that additional organic waste streams would be required to drive the composting process. The needed waste materials were found by reaching out to other area industrial and agricultural developments to determine interest and suitability for organic waste composting. After 5 months of experimenting with various organic wastes, the pilot project concluded by successfully producing a saleable Class "A" compost material.

RESULTS

Building upon the successful pilot project, the composting contractor was motivated to construct a large scale industrial composting facility to support the potato processing plant and several other area developments. Within a few months of operation, the Simplot Canada facility successfully diverted thousands of tons of organic byproducts to the industrial composting facility. The project has greatly reduced the complexity and cost of managing organic byproducts while simultaneously minimizing negative environmental impacts of the operation.

Thinking Outside the Canister for Low-Impact Packaging

Singing Dog Vanilla

OPPORTUNITY

Eugene, Oregon's Singing Dog Vanilla has sustainability at its core. It works directly with vanilla growers and brings organic vanilla to the US market. With its line of Singing Dog Vanilla teas, the company wanted to find sustainable, low-impact packaging. Most tea canisters are made of various metals or hard plastics and bound with toxic glues and dyes. Management searched the market to find an alternative, but was unable to solve this problem with what was currently offered by suppliers.

SOLUTION

Singing Dog Vanilla worked with a Northwest manufacturer to create an ecologically friendly packaging option. Instead of using a metal tube canister, they used cardboard. Their goal was to create an ecologically friendly, high quality product that was still visually appealing. Inside the canister, one bag encases the loose tea leaves and another keeps the tea bag sanitary. Both bags are made from 100% compostable vegetable fiber. The tea bag is also reusable, to minimize waste. The two plastic lids to the container are number 2 recyclable and the tea label was attached with non-toxic adhesive, making the tube compostable as well. The tea leaves, once spent, are also very easily composted.

RESULTS

Singing Dog Vanilla saves over $4,200 for every 1,000 tea canisters they produce by using non-toxic, biodegradable packaging instead of standard metal containers. Overall, it is less expensive and more sustainable than the other options available, and they have successfully created a product that employees at Singing Dog Vanilla, as well as customers, can feel good about.

Shore Power Electricity for Trailer Refrigeration

Organically Grown Company

OPPORTUNITY

Fresh and frozen food products are distributed and delivered in trailers cooled by diesel-powered refrigeration units (a.k.a. reefers). Organically Grown Company (OGC), an employee and grower-owned organic produce distributor, determined they could replace diesel fuel used to cool parked reefer trailers by using electricity. Diesel engines in reefer trailers run for many hours each day while parked during normal operations, including run time to pre-cool the cargo box prior to loading, or during the loading process, and while loaded trailers are staged before delivery. OGC recognized that using **shore power**—a term used to describe the **shore side** electrical power utilized by ships, aircraft, or land-based vehicles while main or auxiliary engines are turned off—was an energy and cost-saving way to eliminate stationary diesel usage in reefers at their main distribution center in Portland, Oregon.

SOLUTION

Organically Grown Company installed specially-designed shore power electric docking stations at 17 loading dock doors to plug-in refrigerated trailers while parked. These shore power docking stations include specialized safety features to automatically de-energize a power cord whenever a plug is disconnected. Docking stations also include self-release connectors to automatically release the plug if a trailer is accidently driven off while still connected. OGC worked with Shorepower Technologies on the design and installation of the shore connection system, and with CleanFuture on implementation.

Fortunately, many of OGC's 23 trailers already had refrigeration units able to run on either diesel or electricity so it was a simple matter of installing a plug receptacle at the rear of their trailers to plug in. All replacement reefers for future acquisitions will be ordered with dual diesel or electric capability specified.

RESULTS

For every $2.30 of diesel consumed in a reefer, the equivalent cost is about $0.70 per operating hour. Savings of $23,000 were achieved in the first year by using electricity, instead of diesel, in parked reefer trailers. Expected second year cost savings are estimated to be about 60% higher, based on higher usage, as well as trailer efficiency modifications being ramped-up and completed in the last 5 months of the first year's operation. This savings is significant for a company which was already limiting parked run time without the benefit of electricity. Plugs were permanently installed at the left rear corner of trailers with wiring running to the refrigeration unit at the front so that short cords make the connection from the dock to the rear of the trailer. OGC was also able to reduce maintenance expenses based on fewer diesel run hours, in addition to the diesel fuel savings. Local air quality benefits are an additional positive result of replacing diesel with electricity; emissions were reduced by 139 metric tons of carbon dioxide (CO_2), 0.93 tons of nitrogen oxides (NOx), 2.19 metric tons of carbon monoxide (CO), 0.03 tons of particulate matter (PM) and 0.02 metric tons of reactive organic gases (ROG) during OGC's first year of operation. Quieter operation with electricity is another side benefit of running refrigeration units on shore power electricity compared to diesel while parked.

District Energy for Food Manufacturers is Energy Efficient and Low Carbon

Boardman Industrial Park.

OPPORTUNITY

Businesses in the Boardman Industrial Park at the Port of Morrow in Oregon benefit from steam supplied by nearby Coyote Springs Cogeneration Plant. Coyote Springs supplies steam through underground pipes to neighboring businesses in district energy. District energy is energy efficient and reliable, typically requiring less capital investment, risk and operational costs than systems where each plant must maintain its own boiler.

SOLUTION

Steam piping installed and owned by the Port of Morrow delivers steam from the Coyote Springs Cogeneration Plant to food manufacturers and other industry in the Boardman Industrial

Park. Five individual businesses contract directly with Portland General Electric, the operator of the Coyote Springs Cogeneration Plant, to purchase their steam requirements. The Port of Morrow provides the distribution infrastructure to deliver steam.

RESULTS

District heating has various advantages compared to individual heating systems. District heating is more energy efficient, due to simultaneous production of heat and electricity in combined heat and power generation plants. This has the added benefit of reducing carbon emissions. The larger combustion units at the cogeneration plant also have a more advanced flue gas cleaning than single boiler systems.

PART THREE
ECONOMIC SUSTAINABILITY

Economic Sustainability is the development of innovative business opportunities, services, and products that produce positive company image and recognition.

—*Northwest Food Processors Sustainability Guide*

INTRODUCING ECONOMIC SUSTAINABILITY

Economic sustainability assures that a company is viable for the long term by managing according to principles that support the environment and the community as well as the company's economic well-being. The sustainable company operates so that its employees, customers, partners, communities, and shareholders all benefit.

Shareholder/stakeholder value is an essential component to the longevity of a business. Incorporating sustainability into strategic planning and business practices can lead to better innovation, competitive advantage, access to new markets, and increased margins or market share.

Innovation is critical to sustaining any enterprise; those that do not innovate eventually disappear. Sustainable innovation seeks to produce new products, services, and processes while efficiently using materials, energy, and labor and reducing waste. In essence, innovation leads to increased productivity, which leads to increased competitiveness and increased profits.

Human capital protection is essential for employee morale and for accessing untapped creative potential. Sustainable companies recognize that employees are their most valuable asset. They understand the importance of encouragement and recognition for positive contributions and of engaging and maintaining a superior workforce.

Partnerships can be an important investment as a company seeks opportunities for economic sustainability. Product and service providers, educational institutions, consultants, government agencies, and non-governmental organizations can be a source of information, solutions, and problem solving. Investigate the resources in your industry cluster, and engage them to assist your company in achieving its sustainability goals.

ENERGY EFFICIENCY MAKES GOOD BUSINESS SENSE

Energy efficiency contributes to economic sustainability in the following ways:

- Energy affects the bottom line; it can be a company's single-largest *uncontrolled* expense.
- Energy efficiency mitigates the impacts of rising energy prices or volatile energy markets.
- Energy efficiency improves productivity, enhances reliability, and improves safety.
- Energy accounts for over 90% of greenhouse gas emissions.
- Incentives and technical assistance are available for energy efficiency projects and O&M.

Because of the importance of energy efficiency, in 2009, NWFPA adopted a goal to reduce industry-wide energy intensity by 25% in 10 years and 50% in 20 years. Access the NWFPA Energy Roadmap at **http://www.nwfpa.org** under Energy.

Questions to Ask

- Does my company actively seek development of new products and processes?
- Does my company have a plan for infrastructure improvement and process investment?
- Does my company have a program for employee engagement, skills training and development, and recognition of contributions?
- What hidden resources, and hidden liabilities, does my company have/
- What potential partners could bring valuable resources to assist our efforts?

Employee-Driven Continuous Improvement

Bellingham Cold Storage

OPPORTUNITY

In 2000, Doug Thomas, Bellingham Cold Storage's president and CEO, started Excellence through Continuous Improvement (ECI), a program that engaged employees in decisions and process improvement at all levels of the organization. An expanded ECI program would further improve productivity, efficiency, and accuracy.

SOLUTION

Bellingham Cold Storage (BCS) implemented Kaizen, an agile and rapid technique to identify processes that seem redundant, require unnecessary hard work, or can be improved to make employee jobs safer and/or more efficient. Kaizen is a Japanese philosophy of continuous improvement of processes in business, management, engineering, and manufacturing. Kaizen (改善) means "change for the better."

Employees place their suggestions for process improvement on Kaizen boards, which are located throughout the plant in the various production areas. Through a team-based process, employees decide whether to implement each suggestion. After teams are assigned to a course of action to implement the suggestion, it is moved from the suggestion side of the Kaizen board to the solution side, which indicates that it is now part of the work routine. When a solution has been fully implemented, it is taken off the board and added to a running list of actions that is renewed every year.

Employees can make as many suggestions as they want. For each idea submitted, employees receive a small cash reward in their paycheck, providing an immediate incentive for sharing ideas. The amount of the cash award is determined based upon the amount of savings to the company that is produced by the idea. Additionally, each year one employee receives an award for having the most Kaizen ideas that year.

RESULTS

BCS has saved almost $250,000 since Kaizen was implemented and has awarded almost $10,000 in cash awards to employees. Employee engagement and satisfaction have increased and quality and productivity have improved as well as company profits.

Community-based On-Site Ammonia Safety Training

Bellingham Cold Storage

OPPORTUNITY

For Bellingham Cold Storage (BCS), the safety of its community comes first. The company is committed to ensuring that anyone who handles anhydrous ammonia knows how to handle and store it properly. Training is required, but the Ammonia Safety Training Institute is located in Watsonville, California and traveling and attendance is cost prohibitive for smaller companies that work with anhydrous ammonia. BCS saw an opportunity to make its community safer by making training more accessible.

SOLUTION

Many companies would not allow competitors on their worksites, but BCS invites any company, including its competitors, working with anhydrous ammonia to attend its safety training. BCS's tenants, fire departments, and any business in Whatcom and Skagit Counties that meets the legal threshold for required training is invited.

RESULTS

Fire departments and company on-site emergency responders are trained side-by-side before an emergency, which helps with communication and flow during a crisis. A side benefit is the intercompany and community relationships that are formed during the training.

Employee Workforce Referral Pipeline

Green Mountain Coffee Roasters, Inc.

OPPORTUNITY

The workforce at Green Mountain Coffee Roaster's Sumner plant more than tripled over a two-year period and is expected to grow by more than 60% within the next two years. A pipeline of highly qualified workers was needed to fill these positions.

SOLUTION

Employees were encouraged to refer prospective employees to the company by the award of a cash bonus when a new hire that they had referred satisfactorily reaches the six-month employment milestone.

RESULTS

Green Mountain is able to tap into the employees' "circle of influence" to build a robust referral pipeline and reduce recruitment costs. Frontline workers are motivated to only refer the best candidates and feel they are contributing to the long-term success of the company.

Communicating the Vision to Employees

Dave's Killer Bread

OPPORTUNITY

Dave's Killer Bread has cultivated a loyal workforce and regularly looks for ways to improve employee satisfaction and morale. An employee survey revealed a desire for more communication between frontline workers and supervisors. The company sought to create a better system to communicate the company vision and direction and encourage employees to share their ideas and suggestions.

SOLUTION

Dave's Killer Bread management initiated quarterly company meetings for each shift. The meetings set context for the company and are structured as questions and answers for employees. Employees are also given time to share their opinions and suggestions for improvements.

In addition, supervisors hold five-minute standing meetings before each shift to set context for the day and to make announcements.

RESULTS

Employees are more committed to the company's overall success because they know and understand how they fit into the overall strategic direction of the company. Standing meetings give employees the opportunity to ask questions, provide feedback, and get issues addressed in real-time, which positively impacts their productivity and quality of work.

Financial Literacy Program Reduces Employee Stress

Green Mountain Coffee Roasters, Inc.

OPPORTUNITY

Green Mountain Coffee Roasters has always been committed to its employee's financial success. Employees can participate in an employee stock purchase plan (ESPP) where they buy company stock at a 15% discounted price through payroll deductions. The company automatically enrolls employees in a 401(k) program in which the company offers a 50% match of the employee contribution up to the 6% maximum deduction.

During the 2000s, the average US employee experienced increased financial stress due to the dramatic increase in home foreclosures and defaults on credit cards. The Federal Reserve has calculated that the average employee spends 28 hours each month worried about, calculating, or stressed over finances, costing employers $5,000 a year per employee in lost productivity.[2]

Green Mountain knew the economic crisis was having an impact on its employees, potentially draining productivity and increasing emotional stress on the job. Green Mountain saw an opportunity to help employees gain financial literacy to meet their short- and long-term financial goals by addressing their financial concerns.

SOLUTION

Employees can enroll in a financial literacy program called Dave Ramsey's Financial Peace University. This program teaches employees and their families how to make the right decisions to achieve financial goals and experience a total money makeover to become debt-free.

RESULTS

When employees feel secure about their personal finances, they are less stressed and so are more productive, happier, healthier, and miss fewer days of work.

Note: Learn more about Dave Ramsey's Financial Peace University at http://www.daveramsey.com.

---

2 "Employee Financial Education," National Financial Educators Council, http://www.financialeducatorscouncil.org/employee-financial-education.html.

A Living Wage for All Employees Boosts Productivity

Dave's Killer Bread

OPPORTUNITY

Frontline workers are challenged to find a job that pays more than minimum wage. Dave's Killer Bread saw an opportunity to create a pay system that was more equitable for all employees.

SOLUTION

Dave's Killer Bread eliminated its annual bonus program and increased all employees' pay to a living wage.

RESULTS

Paying employees a living wage gives them dignity, as they are able to afford basic necessities, without public or private assistance. It decreases financial stress, which improves employee productivity, work quality and morale and reduces absenteeism.

Partner with State Employment Training to Reduce Training Costs and Increase Employee Skills

Sierra Nevada Brewing Co.

OPPORTUNITY

Sierra Nevada Brewing Co.'s growth rates had accelerated over previous years, and with the growing demand, the company experienced a greater need for qualified and technically trained employees to support additional production demands.

SOLUTION

Sierra Nevada worked with the State of California's Employment Training Panel (ETP). This partnership offset the costs of job skills training necessary to maintain a high-performance workplace and strengthen the company's competitive edge. Sierra Nevada now trains its employees in commercial, business, hazardous materials, and management skills. Training is done in conjunction with other departments in two-hour increments.

We have worked under three contracts—the first one successfully ended in November 2012. Two hundred and eight employees successfully reached the 24-hour requirement and together accumulated 6,729 hours of training. Our next contract was not as successful, as our focus and efforts were directed at construction and commissioning of our second brewery in Mills River, North Carolina. Most recently, we have partnered with our local community college and anticipate another successful contract with their revised 8-hour requirement.

Sierra Nevada recently rolled out a learning management system to enable better visibility to training and development for our employees.

RESULTS

Training has resulted in a better-skilled workforce, increased employee satisfaction and loyalty and lower turnover. Cross-departmental training ensures that employees get to know each other and gain a better understanding of the entire production process.

Employee Training Improves Productivity and Employee Retention

Tim's Cascade Chips

OPPORTUNITY

Over the years Tim's Cascade Chips has gone through numerous major acquisitions; most recently, Pinnacle Foods acquired Tim's in 2009. Amidst the natural turmoil caused by significant company changes, Tim's knows it needs to retain its experienced and skilled frontline workers to keep up with increasing demands on productivity and consistently produce the unique kettle-style chips and quality snacks for which Tim's has become famous.

SOLUTION

Tim's gives employees in-depth on-the-job training and also cross-trains them in several positions. For specialized training, Tim's employees can now participate in one of Pinnacle Foods' online learning programs called "Reach Your Peak," which is a suite of learning tools to help employees further develop their knowledge and achieve personal performance goals. To participate, employees and managers co-develop a learning plan using a competency development guide, which helps managers track the professional development of their staff. Employees have continuous opportunities to improve their skills by taking advantage of new opportunities, such as assisting in training new hires or delivering quarterly trainings for all employees.

RESULTS

Production is steadily growing between 10 to 15% per year, and accidents have decreased by 9.4% over a five-year period. Cross-training ensures that Tim's maintains high quality and predictable output per hour, as employees are able to work on different production lines.

Mechanical Separation of Packaging from Food Wastes allows Recycling and Eliminates Disposal Fees.

Pacific Foods of Oregon, Inc.

OPPORTUNITY

Pacific Foods, a producer of all natural and organic foods, adopted a goal of zero waste to landfill, where discard materials are minimized or reused and all remaining wastes are recycled or composted. In 2006, Pacific Foods adopted recycling rate as a key performance indicator and by 2007, it was recovering 40% of its wastes.

However, much of the waste going to landfill went via a large, highly visible, and messy compactor that took waste from the production lines. A waste sort conducted by Portland State University's Community Environmental Services revealed that 95% of this waste was food-contaminated packaging material. Manually separating the product from the packaging was cost-prohibitive, so all of this waste—50 tons or more in a typical month—went to landfill.

THE SOLUTION

Pacific Foods designed and constructed, at a cost of over $100,000, a customized "de-packing" station that mechanically separates the unsellable product from the packaging. This eliminated a considerable flow of waste to the landfill. Packaging materials are now being recycled and Pacific Foods is exploring options to divert the food residuals to anaerobic digestion or other beneficial uses.

BENEFITS

The company's recycling rate jumped from 40% in 2007 to 88% in August 2011, the month Pacific Foods "retired" its garbage compactor (complete with a retirement party, as featured in this funny spoof of *The Office*: please see http://www.youtube.com/watch?v=A9T05pkAErg). In 2012, the recycling operation saved over $100,000 in disposal fees and generated approximately $65,000 in revenue—financial benefits that help to justify the full-time employment of four recycling specialists.

In-sourcing Ingredients Improves Quality and Engages Employees

Standing Stone Brewing Company

OPPORTUNITY

Since its founding, Standing Stone Brewing Company has looked for ways to operate its brewery and restaurant that protect and restore the environment and support the health and happiness of its community, guests, and employees. In addition to sourcing its ingredients as locally as possible, Standing Stone saw an opportunity to "insource" its ingredients from its own farming operations and engage its employees in new and unforeseen ways.

SOLUTION

In 2011, the company leased nearby farmland and is now producing its own eggs and beef as well as raising other animals on the farm. Rather than hiring a professional farmer, Standing Stone asked a neighboring farmer to help train the company's staff. A rotating handful of employees now work at the farm in the early morning hours composting, feeding chickens and cows, moving fences, and collecting eggs for the restaurant.

RESULTS

The company has seen reduced costs and improved product quality. In addition, the enthusiasm that Standing Stone employees gain from helping to bring organic food from the farm directly onto customers' plates often spills over into conversations with customers, which is great publicity for the company.

Onsite Agriculture Supplies High Quality and Sustainable Raw Materials

Sierra Nevada Brewing Co.

OPPORTUNITY

Beer is made of four primary ingredients: barley, hops, yeast, and water. Because Sierra Nevada Brewing Co. relies so heavily on agricultural products, the company was interested to learn as much as possible about the crops used as well as some of the barriers to moving toward more sustainable farming practices. Sierra Nevada also has a very successful onsite restaurant that is one of the most popular restaurants in Chico, California. The company strives to serve the most fresh, local, and organic ingredients possible—and how much closer can you get than onsite?

SOLUTION

Sierra Nevada maintains eleven acres of hop field, 120 acres of barley and a two-acre garden for their restaurant in Chico, CA. All of these fields are certified organic by Oregon Tilth.

RESULTS

The hop and barley fields are harvested and used to brew Sierra Nevada's Estate Harvest IPA. This beer is the company's only certified organic beer and is made with ingredients straight from its fields. The restaurant garden yields year-round produce and herbs that are as fresh as they could possibly be – more than 31,000 pounds of fresh ingredients in 2014! These fields also receive compost that is made onsite from discarded food and other organic discards from the brewing process, creating an elegant closed-loop program.

Employees learn about farming practices and have a greater connection and appreciation for the farmers that supply raw materials. This creates a fantastic story for consumers.

Biodiesel from Spent Vegetable Oil Offsets Petroleum Fuels Use

Sierra Nevada Brewing Co.

OPPORTUNITY

One of the guiding sustainability approaches at Sierra Nevada Brewing Co. is to close resource loops whenever possible. This requires the brewery to look at what is leaving its facility and what is coming in. The goal is to recover resources that are leaving and find a way to bring them back into plant operations. One of these resources that was leaving was used vegetable oil from the onsite restaurant. One of the resources that is consumed is fuel for the company's fleet.

SOLUTION

In 2008, Sierra Nevada investigated biodiesel production using the spent vegetable oil from its restaurant. The brewery purchased a BioPro 190 biodiesel processor in February of that year and began biodiesel production. The processor is capable of handling 50-gallon batches of used vegetable oil and processing it into biodiesel in 48 hours. Sierra Nevada's restaurant produces roughly 50 gallons of spent vegetable oil every week and the machine is able to process the restaurant's entire output. Sierra Nevada paid $9,000 for the machine and received a $1,000 tax credit. The machine paid for itself in about 18 months and the biodiesel now costs the company about $1.70 per gallon to make. The finished biodiesel is used in Sierra Nevada's fleet of trucks to offset petroleum fuel consumption.

RESULTS

Since purchasing the machine, Sierra Nevada has processed 15,750 gallons of spent vegetable oil into alternative fuel for their fleet. This has reduced greenhouse gas emissions, reduced dependence on petroleum fuel, avoided disposal costs of spent vegetable oil, created a job/task, and is a shining closed-loop story to share with consumers.

On-site Electric Vehicle Charging Stations

Sierra Nevada Brewing Co.

OPPORTUNITY

In early 2009, Sierra Nevada Brewing Co. was approached by a local electric car dealer asking if the company would install electric vehicle charging stations. Sierra Nevada owner Ken Grossman knew that if technology like electric vehicles is going to be feasible in their community, the infrastructure for those technologies needs to be in place. For this reason, Ken agreed to install public charging stations, hoping it would help the technology catch on in the Chico, California community.

SOLUTION

Sierra Nevada installed two level 2 Charge Point (formerly Coulomb) electric vehicle charging stations in its public parking lot in April 2009. The chargers are tied directly to Sierra Nevada's solar array that covers the parking lot where vehicles can be charged using a renewable source of electricity. The chargers at the facility are offered free to anyone driving an electric vehicle to the brewery—employees, vendors, and guests. Sierra Nevada paid a total of $3,000 for the two chargers with network monitoring.

RESULTS

The chargers sat idle until 2011 when the Nissan Leaf came on the market and are now used by several local electric vehicle drivers in the community as well as guests visiting the Chico area.

The installation of the charging station shows company commitment to the future, promotes the use of alternative fuel, encourages reduction in petroleum consumption, and improves customer relations.

Green Teams Drive Recycling Program Successes

New Seasons Market

OPPORTUNITY

In 2007, New Seasons implemented a highly successful recycling and composting program, called "Waste to Worth," in all of its groceries stores. New Seasons management knew that the success of the program was dependent upon employees' enthusiasm and passion for implementing sustainable practices and the ability to drive costs savings through the identification of waste-reducing best practices specific to each department.

SOLUTION

New Seasons piloted its first Green Team at one store by identifying a "green champion" and other store employees who believed their store could do better. The success of that pilot led company management to support and encourage expansion of the model to all store locations.

As in the pilot, the New Seasons sustainability manager and each store manager identified an employee or group of employees passionate about reducing their store's environmental impact and then built the Green Teams around their leadership.

Green Team Basics

- Each store must have a Green Team which includes at least one staff member from each department.
- Teams get up to 40 hours of paid time to choose a community service project each year.
- The teams meet for 30 to 60 minutes each month and are paid for that time.

RESULTS

Every New Seasons store recycles and composts, resulting in a 50% reduction in overall garbage and conversion of 2,140 tons of organic waste to compost. Composting saves New Seasons Market 30% compared to landfill costs, which amounted to more than $25,000 in 2011. The Green Teams have increased employee professional development and leadership opportunities and improved employee loyalty and satisfaction.

Annual Energy Program Assessments and Awards Boost Achievement

Darigold, Inc.

OPPORTUNITY

Darigold operates 11 plants across the Pacific Northwest, with a range of products including milk powder, cheese, whey, butter, milk, cottage cheese, and more. These plants differ in size and in products produced, which introduces challenges for energy management at the corporate level. Each plant has an Energy Team— a cross-functional group that meets monthly to discuss energy management at the plant and how they can improve. The team's plan and meeting minutes are shared with the corporate Energy Engineer. Energy use is monitored and recorded in a monthly report covering every facility that are sent to plant managers, senior directors, and the VP of operations. The reports also include Energy Team meeting minutes and a list of action items for energy efficiency improvement. Darigold measures energy intensity in BTUs per pound of product to help standardize comparisons between plants. But Darigold needed a way to further measure the success of its Energy Teams, since the Ingredients Division uses far more energy per pound than the Consumer Products Division.

SOLUTION

At the beginning of every fiscal year, Darigold performs an objective evaluation of each plant's energy team, and invites utilities and other partners to join. These "Energy Program Assessments" are comprehensive evaluations more advanced than basic scorecards used in assessing the efficacy of an energy management program, since they focus on how a facility can improve. Each assessment participant scores criteria independently, and provides suggestions on how the plant can improve its score for next year based on what they observed and inquired about during the comprehensive plant tour. Bringing in outside partners for the assessment is unique and allows for new eyes, a fresh perspective, and an unbiased view of the Energy Teams' hard work.

RESULTS

Darigold has made progress toward its goal to reduce its company-wide energy intensity by 25% in 10 years, and some plants have already reached that goal. After 4 years of performing Energy Program Assessments, Darigold has seen that the plants with high assessment scores are also the most successful in energy intensity reductions. Annual awards recognize efforts and achievements. The plants with the highest annual energy savings and the highest Energy Program Assessment scores receive a "Green Light Award," each member of the Energy Team gets an all-weather jacket, and all plant employees receive a lunch cooler with "Energy Champion" embroidered on it.

Photos Raise Employee Awareness of Waste Reduction Opportunities

Lamb Weston

OPPORTUNITY

Lamb Weston has organized "Green Teams" across its facilities. These cross-functional groups work on improving each plant's energy efficiency, waste production, and embark on other sustainability initiatives. Engaging a large workforce and creating greater awareness of sustainability opportunities is a challenge, especially in a very busy processing environment.

SOLUTION

In May 2014, one Lamb Weston Green Team developed a "What's a Picture Worth?" program to raise awareness and engage employees in the hunt for opportunities to eliminate waste. The purpose of this activity was to bring general awareness to overlooked waste as well as to provide a visual record of waste reduction opportunities. The Green Team divided into three groups: Energy Waste, Water Waste, and Recycling Opportunities. Each group was given a camera to use as they walked through the facility, taking pictures of waste when identified. The photos were then shared with all of the Green Team members and prioritized by greatest opportunity. Photos were also posted on bulletin boards to help communicate with all plant teams. Maintenance work orders were developed to eliminate or reduce energy and water waste, and improved employee education on recycling was introduced for proper material handling.

RESULTS

Over 90 images were captured during this team effort, directly influencing work orders and projects to eliminate waste and conserve energy and water. The activity increased employee engagement throughout the plant and brought awareness to waste. While cost savings are ongoing, this facility has not quantified them as yet, but has focused more on the behavior change that the project has driven. Team members better understand the necessity to call out waste as it occurs versus going about their day to day work activities and not bringing any improvement opportunities forward. With sustainability, no opportunity is too small. But without engagement and awareness, often times waste occurs but is not identified because employees lack education on what a waste reduction opportunity looks like.

Celebrating Wins and Communicating Success through Videos

J.R. Simplot Company

OPPORTUNITY

In 2009, Northwest Food Processors Association adopted a goal to reduce industry-wide energy intensity by 25% within 10 years, and by 50% in 20 years. That year, JR Simplot Company's CEO signed a pledge to reduce energy intensity by 25% in 10 years. Simplot's Corporate Energy group began working with industrial sites, implementing energy efficiency projects, making factory upgrades, and other measures to reduce the large company's overall energy intensity. This effort became known as "25 x 10"—shorthand for the energy reduction goal. Many employees thought the goal was unattainable and that Simplot would not be able to fulfill its pledge. And many employees were not aware of Simplot's sustainable accomplishments. Simplot needed a means to communicate its successes and to recognize those employees responsible for these successes.

SOLUTION

Simplot's Corporate Energy group decided to hire a contractor to develop videos each time an industrial site met its 25 x 10 goal. These 3-5 minute videos would highlight the people involved in the energy intensity reduction and how they improved operations at the site. These videos serve as tangible evidence that the company can attain its energy intensity reduction goals and helps make employees aware of the company's sustainable accomplishments. Recognizing employee efforts engages employees and drives further success.

RESULTS

As of August 2016, nine locations have met the 25 x 10 goal and eight videos have been developed and shared internally with Simplot employees. The video demonstrates that these plants have achieved their energy intensity reductions in short amounts of time, and some have exceeded the 25% goal. The videos also show that many projects have benefits beyond energy efficiency— such as improved productivity and safety, reductions in water use, and reductions in greenhouse gas emissions. At the end of August 2015, Simplot's North American Food Group has reduced its energy intensity by about 19%.

Fair Game, Fair Match, Fair Trade+

Singing Dog Vanilla

OPPORTUNITY

After deciding to start a vanilla company in 2004, the co-owners of Singing Dog Vanilla had to determine where and from whom to source vanilla beans. While there were many choices for moderately inexpensive beans, co-owners Marty and Bill wanted more than just vanilla. They sought out the best source for high quality vanilla from friendly farmers with whom they could establish a strong, long-lasting relationship.

SOLUTION

Marty and Bill decided to form a Fair Trade Plus partnership with farmers they had connected with in Papua, New Guinea and Indonesia. Most Fair Trade purchasing models only pay a fair value for goods at the point of purchase. But Singing Dog Vanilla not only pays for the vanilla beans outright, they also pay the farmers a percentage of the money made from vanilla product sales. This partnership helps to bring economic growth to the villages that the farmers live in, and their happiness means everything to Singing Dog.

RESULTS

The Fair Trade Plus partnership enriches the social and economic sustainability of both Singing Dog Vanilla and its farmer partners. The company receives high quality beans and the farmers receive fair payment for their hard work. Further, they do not need to sell to additional buyers or pick unripe beans in order to make enough money. The partnership has created a strong bond between the farmers and the management at Singing Dog Vanilla. Bill travels to Indonesia every year to visit the partner farmers and maintain this crucial relationship. Despite the current worldwide vanilla shortage, Singing Dog Vanilla has secured its vanilla supply for pre-existing customers on a bulk scale, and new customers on a retail scale (economic sustainability), simultaneously ensuring the happiness and viability of their partners in Papua, New Guinea and Indonesia (social responsibility).

Screen Displays Provide Real-Time Energy Monitoring for Production Personnel

Darigold, Inc.

OPPORTUNITY

Studies show that when people have access to data on their energy use, they make better decisions to conserve energy. When energy consumption is monitored by monthly reports or monthly utility statements, it is difficult to manage energy use after-the-fact. The challenge was to inform front-line production employees about real-time energy consumption so that they could manage energy use with production.

SOLUTION

Darigold's Chehalis plant installed an energy information system to monitor and track real-time energy use. As part of the system, large-screen displays were installed to show real-time energy use and promote energy conservation. The purpose was to make energy use visible to employees so they could manage the use with production.

The energy information system makes use of two electric meters, five gas flow meters, and two steam flow meters placed at various stages in the manufacturing process. Two meters were also installed to measure production output to correlate energy use with production in real-time. Four monitors were placed throughout the plant, in the control room, lunch room, boiler room and office area. The constant visibility keeps employees informed and interested in energy use on the production line.

RESULTS

Engaging a large workforce and creating greater awareness of sustainability opportunities is a challenge, especially in a very busy processing environment. Darigold was able to find a way to involve and inform employees of real-time energy use. As a result they can proactively manage real-time energy use along with production output and assess immediate impacts.

CRES-Certified Employees Drive Efficient Equipment Operations and Energy Savings

Lamb Weston

OPPORTUNITY

In September 2013, a Lamb Weston frozen potato facility wanted to identify low cost/no capital opportunities to conserve energy and improve processes while at the same time improve awareness of the human behavioral impact on equipment operation and its subsequent tie to energy use. Management worked with the Northwest Energy Efficiency Alliance and Cascade Energy to discover ways to promote behavioral energy efficiency.

SOLUTION

Two Lamb Weston refrigeration operators earned the designation of Certified Refrigeration Energy Specialist (CRES) through a hands-on training program. The program included home-site assignment and classroom work, which led to a broader understanding of system energy consumption. CRES training highlights the behavioral impact of equipment operation, which led to the site making changes in operational practices, system training materials, and scheduled maintenance work streams. With a pay-it-forward approach, the two trained team members then shared key learnings with other teams operating other systems in the facility and together they identified and implemented additional energy savings projects.

RESULTS

Improvements made through project work and increased awareness and education on efficient equipment operation resulted in a 2% reduction in electricity use. The certification empowered team members to become more effective in recognizing and capturing energy savings in refrigeration—the facility's highest energy consumption system.

www.ingramcontent.com/pod-product-compliance
Lightning Source LLC
Chambersburg PA
CBHW070234190526
45169CB00001B/180